Belize: Human Smuggling, Transnational Organised Crime, Politicians And Public Servants

DAURIUS FIGUEIRA

© DAURIUS FIGUEIRA 2018

Table of Contents

Introduction

This is an analysis of the power relations between transnational organised crime (TOC), ruling politicians of Belize and public servants of the Immigration and Naturalisation Department (IND), Ministry of Immigration, Belize. This relationship was revealed in the audit report of the Auditor General of Belize of the IND titled: "Special Audit-Visa Immigration and Nationality Department for the period 2011-2013" and the press reports of the hearings Special Senate Committee in its investigation of the contents of the said audit report. This analysis focuses on the alliance between TOC, ruling politicians and public servants in the creation and operation of an illicit organised crime enterprise located within the operational space of a licit/legal state agency, the IND. The illicit enterprise is human smuggling on a globalised scale driven by TOC in its quest for licit/legal visas, permanent residency permits, nationality certificates, passports and other forms of identification of Belize for its clients of global origin. Specifically, the emphasis is on the power relations of the three major entities of the alliance that make possible the illicit organised crime enterprise focused on the IND of Belize. The dynamic of this alliance and its impact upon the members of the alliance, the state of Belize, the governance of Belize and the people of Belize are all illustrated and even expressed by the power relations between members of the alliance and the discourses utilised in the exercise of these power/force relations.

The discourse of corruption now widely utilised to explain the dysfunctional nature of post-independence states of the British colonial Caribbean has been found wanting to explain the dynamics of the power relations under scrutiny in this analysis. As it fails to grapple with the genesis and operational reality of the state founded on the Westminster model and its pervasive inability to respond to challenges posed to its monopoly on violence throughout the post-independence states of the British colonial Caribbean. The discourse of corruption can only focus on its premise that the problem lies in the failings of those charged with managing the agencies of the state on a daily basis. And it relentlessly seeks this out, blind to the need to grapple with the issue of the organic origin and formation of the state and the operational terrain this state demands for its operational efficiency and potency. The discourse of corruption cannot grasp the fact that the state form of the Westminster model is not organic to the British colonial Caribbean social order on which it was transplanted to/grafted on at the time of independence. A study of this European state form transplanted to the Caribbean utilising the works of Michel Foucault (especially Foucault's discourse of Governmentality and Biopolitics) shows that there is a grave discordance between our social order and the social order of the state form grafted on to our social order with independence. What the state form demands for optimal performance is not provided by our specific social order hence we operate a state form that is weak, emaciated showing all the symptoms of arrested development: A Frankenstein monster even a Dr Jekyll and Mr Hyde. This state form is then gravely challenged to defend itself against the depredations of globalised transnational organised crime as illustrated with the case of the IND of Belize in this study.

The abiding lesson of the study is that the actions of the ruling politicians as described by the discourse of political corruption as those of the public servants of Belize is the hegemonic discourse used in Belize for this purpose. But the instruments and mechanisms they both utilise in their corrupt practises are those of an organised crime enterprise as there are more than one person involved, there is organizational structure, a policed order and the distribution within the organisational structure of the proceeds of the illicit enterprise. Many of these organised crime enterprises encompassing ruling politicians and public servants are located and operate within the spaces of government Ministries serve transnational organised crime groups in Belize via an operational alliance. There can then be no intervention towards mitigation in this operational terrain without the realisation that the reality is operationally a transnational organised enterprise located in the heart of the executive of Belize. The discourse of corruption cannot visualise, gaze upon, understand nor deal with this reality effectively. In Belize the reality of political and other state based corruption has to be assaulted from the position of a Racketeer and Influenced and Corrupt Organisations Act specifically constructed for the operational reality of political and state corruption in Belize at this time. The traditional measures applied in Belize address an operational reality alien to

Belize hence their failure to deal with the problem especially the impunity the operatives of these transnational organised crime enterprises enjoy and wield.

References

For Michel Foucault's analysis of the Western European state form see the following.

Foucault, Michel (2003): "Society Must Be Defended" Picador USA

Foucault, Michel (2007): "Security, Territory, Population" Palgrave USA

Foucault, Michel (2008): "The Birth of Biopolitics" Palgrave USA

Foucault, Michel (1979): "Discipline and Punish" Peregrine USA

CHAPTER 1
Organised Crime, Politicians and Public Servants

The Auditor General of Belize carried out an audit of the Immigrant and Nationality Department (IND) of the Government of Belize for the period 2011-2013. The findings of this audit named: "Special Visa and Other Findings Report on the Immigration and Nationality Department for period January 1, 2012-September 30, 2013" was presented to the Prime Minister Dean Barrow of Belize by way of letter dated May 31, 2016. The said audit report was also placed online. This analysis will focus on the nationality of persons listed in the audit report of having received valid Belizean visas, permanent residency status and Belizean passports illicitly as this illustrates the strategy of organised crime to obtain licit Belizean visas, and nationality documents as revealed in the audit report.

The audit report in Table 1 lists 28 individuals who were issued visas, then Belizean nationality and passports although they didn't qualify for the Belizean nationality and passports. Persons from China accounted for 20 individuals listed on Table 1 out of 28 or 71.42%. Ukraine and Russia were next with 2 individuals each followed by Lebanon, India, Saudi Arabia and the USSR with 1 each. Persons from China overwhelmingly dominated this category. Three successful applicants without sponsors listed on their applications each had a letter dated January 29, 2013 written by Minister Erwin Contreras in their favour to the Director of the Immigrant and Nationality Department.

Table A.1 lists 15 individuals who received visas then permanent residency status thereafter in contravention of the Policy and Procedure Manual. These 15 individuals received permanent residency status which they didn't qualify for. All of the 15 individuals were from China.

Table B lists seven successful applications for visas supported by government ministers. The seven visas were issued without the necessary supporting documents supplied. At the Belize North Border Station (BNBS) there were three successful applicants listed: two from Honduras supported by the intervention of Hugo Patt and one from Paraguay supported by Elvin Penner. At the Philip Goldson International Airport (PGIA) 4 applicants were successful two from India and two from Nepal all supported by Edmond Castro.

Table C lists the details of the nine visa stubs from the Belize West Border Station (BWBS) that were missing hence unavailable for the audit. The visas were issued to nine applicants with their countries of origin as follows: Colombia 2, Japan 2, Salvador 2, Singapore 1, South Korea 1 and Nicaragua 1. The audit report states that 8 visa foils were stolen and sold to officials of the Belize City Council. Even before recovery of the 8 visas officials of the Belize IND decided to issue these visas but without the visa stickers/foils in order to earn revenue and not lose it by discarding these visas. But the audit states that 134 visa stubs were not presented for audit nor on hand at the Belize North Border Station (BNBS) and Philip Godson International Airport (PGIA) stations. Which points to an operational reality common to the Belize IND during the period of the audit. It's noteworthy that of the 134 missing stubs 1 was cancelled with 133 visas issued on these stubs 62 missing stubs or 46.26% were issued to Russians, 25 to Japanese with the remaining 46 to a wide range of nationalities as Honduras and El Salvador 7 each, Chinese 6, Colombia 5, South Korea 4, Montenegro and Serbia 2 each. It is apparent from this table the nature of the flow of persons into Belize and the fact that members of transnational organised crime groups can utilise this flow given the operational weaknesses of the Belize IND highlighted in the audit report.

Two visa applicants from China used the same passport size photograph for their visa applications which were approved on July 24, 2013 and two visas issued the same day without the Director's approval and signature on the two application forms. The visa applications of both Chinese applicants were recommended by Minister John Saldivar.

Five Cuban nationals incarcerated at the Belize Central Prison were granted visas to stay in Belize upon their release from prison in spite of the fact that all five presented copies not the original of their Cuban passports. Four of the five

Cubans presented references with their visa applications but these references were not attached to their approved visa applications.

Eight hundred and thirty-three (833) applicants used their US Visas or US Permanent Residence Cards to obtain Belize visas from the Belmopan Station (BMPS), BNBS, BWBS and PGIA in keeping with stated regulations of the Belize IND. The audit report states that 18 persons with expired US visas were granted Belize visas. Of the 18 persons approved for Belize visas 8 were Chinese. The audit report states that there was no evidence that the veracity of the US visas and the US permanent residence cards were verified before the Belize visas were issued. The report states that 7 persons were granted Belize visas on the basis of expired US permanent residence cards. Much more important the audit report states that there is no evidence that persons granted Belize visas on the basis of having a US visa whose country of origin triggered the need to have a DINS and security clearance check done of the applicant were the DINS check and the security clearance done. A Russian female applicant is granted a Belize visa on the basis of being in possession of a US visa but on the application form no proof of this is attached to the said form.

Visa application forms were processed, approved and Belize visas issued even though the applicant didn't sign the visa application form at the BMPS, BNBS, BWPS and PGIA. Applications for visas were approved and issued even though these applications carried no passport size photograph of the applicant. Visas were issued on applications where a photocopy of the photograph of the applicant was attached. Visas were issued at BMPS, BNBS, BWBS and PGIP where the application forms didn't have a photocopy of the bio page of the applicants' native passport attached.

The salient issue that arises so far in the order of presentation of the audit report is the security and veracity of the immigration and naturalisation process of Belize. The possibility exists and is real as a result that you have persons holding Belizean visas, permanent residence status, Belizean nationality and a passport who are not whom and what they say they are! What has been described so far is an apparatus manipulated by agents of the Belizean state that facilitates human smuggling through Belize as a transnational organised crime illicit enterprise. This is an apparatus of power on which the power relations between agents of the state of Belize, the politicians of Belize and transnational organised crime are exercised thereby giving life to the mechanisms of power between the players. This power relation in turn supports a hierarchical edifice of organised crime where the bottom feeders are always on the alert to feed off the stragglers of the edifice. Commanding the apex of this hierarchical order are the Mexican Transnational Trafficking Organisations (MTTOs) with their partners as the snakeheads of China and their affiliates the gangland coyotes of the trade in humans in Central and South America.

What is apparent is that the apparatus accommodates requests by clients who are seeking bona fide legal Belizean immigration and naturalisation documentation. But there is a diversity of demand ranging from the request for visas alone to enter Belize for express purposes, there is the demand for visas that rapidly evolve to the receipt of permanent residence status and there is the demand for rapid naturalisation and the issuing of a Belizean passport. The demand for these documents regardless of the eligibility of the applicant is what drives the demand side of the apparatus. A demand side that is then an illicit enterprise seeking the services of agents of the state to provide a licit service. The demand side of the apparatus given the level of services sought from agents of the state insists on the utilisation of organised crime especially transnational organised crime to create and maintain this illicit enterprise sustainably. The demand side is defined by a price range for services which is influenced by the service offered and its severity in terms of breaches to the relevant body of law and the nature of demand for the range of possible services. The premier package will then involve the granting of a visa then permanent residence culminating in the granting of Belizean nationality and a passport in rapid succession in contravention of law. The demand for specific packages then depends on having the resources to afford any said package and the strategic need for a said package. But in the spaces created by the apparatus other players not affiliated to hegemonic transnational organised crime will constantly seek to play in the field of this licit/illicit enterprise with specific power relations between the hegemonic player and these small players. These power relations inject violence as a given within these spaces.

The agents of the state operating within the spaces of the apparatus are called upon to respond to two opposed realms of power relations: the realm rooted in law and organisational power relations and the illicit realm rooted in an illicit enterprise where violence is a given and the basis of discipline. These involved agents of the state operate in at minimum two diametrically opposed worldviews which render them bi-polar at the level of worldviews, perception and action. The common mechanism to cope with this reality is to use the pursuit of self- interest as the cement of the matrix. The reality is that the apparatus is not sustainable as with the passage of time the agents of the state pursue paths of action which threaten the very sustainability of the apparatus whilst the clients demand volumes of licit documents that threaten the very survival of the apparatus as greed pervades both sides of the equation coupled with fear of retribution and the collapse of the feeding trough.

In its pursuit of its personal agenda in a bi-polar perceptual terrain agents of the state present the gravest threat to the state. As they cannot exclude persons who present threats to the state when they are clients of the illicit business partners of the agents of the state. The agents of the state active in the illicit enterprise must fail to exercise the power granted to them by the state to safeguard the security of the state in the interest of the illicit enterprise when a client of the illicit business is involved. The rule is those who present threats who are not clients of the illicit business it's open season on them which allows the agents of the state to indicate to the social order that they are in fact doing their job. The state then becomes reliant on the vetting of clients by the transnational organised crime group as clients bent on attacking the state are bad for business. But what about the smaller, bottom feeder groups who have no such qualms? It's business as usual! The lesson is then grave as there is no permissible tolerance level for such illicit enterprises as inevitably the safety of the state is challenged. But what if the politicians of the state are also involved in the illicit enterprise? Then the change agent is compromised and the state and social order become trapped in a terrain where the spaces under the control of the state become steadily eroded. The state is progressively weakened, it loses its monopoly on violence and its hegemony is openly challenged. In this condition its ruling elites are noted for impotence in the face of the threats to the state and the institutions of the state become trapped in institutional inertia which stymies the evolution of the state in response to threats to the state. Threats which it must grapple with and mitigate if it's to maintain its hegemony over the social order.

The audit report continued with presenting its findings which exposed the extent the agents of the state were operationally willing to go to facilitate the illicit enterprise of human smuggling. The findings that dealt with breaches of the regulations governing sponsors of applicants for visas exposed the depth of the facilitation process illustrating the nature of the illicit enterprise.

Visas were issued at BMPS, BNBS, BWBS and PGIA to applicants even though there were no required letters of financial support from sponsors attached. This letter is a declaration of the sponsor as to the relationship between the sponsor and applicant, the ability of the sponsor to financially support the applicant during her/his stay in Belize, the income of the sponsor and the legal status of the sponsor in Belize: a citizen of Belize. The audit report states that 3,791 applications presented to the audit team at BMPS, BWBS, BNBS, and PGIA had no letter of financial support attached. In Table K of the audit report lists the names of four sponsors who submitted incomplete letters of financial support for applicants. Three of the applicants are from China and one from India. The three sponsors of the applicants from China have Chinese names and the sponsor for the applicant from India has a South Asian name. What must also be noted is the number of applicants for visas these four sponsors were sponsoring which suggests an enterprise.

Applicants were issued visas at BMPS, BNBS, BWBS and PGIA with proof of the source of funds by their sponsors missing from their application. Bank statements, bank books, cash and credit cards and employment letters from the sponsors were all absent from these successful visa applications. Business certificates, and trade licenses were used and accepted by the immigration officers at BMPS, BNBS, BWBS and PGIA as proof of the financial ability of sponsors. The audit report states that no proof was found that these documents were in fact confirmed as being valid and the audit discovered that visas were issued on the basis of fake documents. A total of 40 applicants with their sponsors were listed in the report as having failed to submit proof of source of funds. There were sponsors listed who were sponsors of multiple applicants.

Of the 40 applicants, 34 were from China and their sponsors all had Chinese names. The remaining 6 comprised 2 applicants from Syria, 1 from Honduras, 1 from Nicaragua, 1 from Brazil and 1 from South Korea. In addition, fake documents and bogus businesses were used by specific sponsors to sponsor multiple successful applicants for visas. This is a potent indicator of organised crime and its power relation with the Belize IND. The list of those sponsors who used a bogus business to sponsor applicants comprised 2 sponsors with Chinese names who sponsored multiple applicants with Chinese names as follows: One sponsored 8 applicants and the other 6. The third and final sponsor listed sponsored 4 applicants with Arabic names with the name of the sponsor also being Arabic. There were three sponsors listed who used fake/bogus certificates to sponsor applicants two of the three had Chinese names and the third had a South Asian name. One sponsor with a Chinese name sponsored 12 applicants with Chinese names whilst the other sponsor with a Chinese name sponsored 7 applicants with Chinese names. The third sponsor who had a South Asian name sponsored 4 applicants with South Asian names. The report lists those sponsors who presented business certificates as a certificate of registration and a trade license that didn't exist in the Belize Company Registry. There were four sponsors listed with three having Chinese names and one with a South Asian name. Those sponsors with Chinese names sponsored only applicants with Chinese names and the sponsor with the South Asian name sponsored applicants only with South Asian names. The three sponsors with Chinese names sponsored a total of 17 applicants with Chinese names and the sponsor with the South Asian name sponsored 2 applicants. Transnational organised crime involved in human smuggling into Belize has now tapped into the market for forged official documents thereby expanding the market for and by extension the level of illicit activity on the market for fake/counterfeit official Belizean documents necessary for the illicit trade in humans.

The report highlighted the failure of the BMPS to retain in its records copies of documents of all applicants for fixed periods of stay in Belize. This was also the case at BNBS, BWBS and PGIA. This void created in the records therefore facilitates the illicit enterprise and is necessary to the attempt to maintain some semblance of lawful operational standard to ensure the illicit enterprise is sustainable. But the daily operation of the illicit enterprise within a licit state agency breeds impunity and breaches of operational methodology multiply even though they are not strategically necessary to the sustainability of the illicit enterprise. This is highlighted in the audit report by the reports of officers not signing and dating applications, not certifying that copies of documents are in fact true copies and not utilising official questionnaires or attaching them to applications. Impunity breeds threats to the state as it does to illicit enterprises provided that those with the powers of state oversight must be willing to intervene to retrieve the situation. The reality described in the audit report is a Belize IND in a feeding frenzy as agents of the state are in pursuit of maximising their take from the illicit enterprise by monetising all requests made for their services. There is then no strategic selectivity which means that tension soon arises between agents of the state and transnational organised crime where transnational organised crime will utilise specific methods to ensure compliance by rogue agents of the state. The apex of the range of solutions isn't necessarily murder as there exists a range of potent threats that flow from the public exposure of the involvement of the agent of the state in the illicit enterprise and the fallout thereof. Usually the certainty of a graphic death at the hands of El Sicario is quite effective.

At the time of the audit nationals of the following countries required a DINS and Security clearance be done having applied for a visa: Afghanistan, Algeria Bangladesh, Bolivia, Colombia, Eritrea, Iran, Iraq, Kenya, Korea (North), Libya, Pakistan, Palestine, Somalia and Sudan. Visas were approved for nationals of these countries without the necessary DINS and Security clearance being done. The audit team was informed that persons of the listed countries in possession of a valid US visa were automatically granted a Belize visa. The veracity of the US visa was not confirmed through US channels. This reality then presents the gravest threat to Belize as an illicit enterprise joined at the hip with a licit state agency has compromised the security apparatus that the Belize IND is charged with policing.

To maintain the integrity of the process of the Belize IND the stock of blank and used visas must be secured and there must be oversight of the system. The audit report stated that at the BMPS, BNBS and BWBS the stock of blank and used visas were not stored in safes but in cabinets. No evidence was forthcoming to the audit team that the Officers in Charge/Port Commanders regularly audited the visa foils, the visa registers and the cash books. No evidence was forthcoming that personnel of the Ministry of Labour, Immigration and Nationality regularly audited the stock of visas held at the stations. No evidence was forthcoming that the Director of Immigration and Nationality on an ongoing basis monitored her/his staff at the BMPS, BNBS, BWBS and PGIA. According to the audit report oversight where it exists is weak and ineffective where it does not it's business as usual. Which resulted in the position of the report that internal controls were very weak at BMPS, BNBS, BWBS and PGIA. On the issuance and control of blank passports and Meryl Sheets the audit report states: "We noted that internal control was very weak when it came to the control and issuance of Blank Passports and the management of Meryl Sheets. It is evident that the Department lacks management in planning, control and organization of vital documents." The Department is then in an operational condition that renders it incapable of repulsing the threat posed by transnational organised crime in Belize. The operational condition of the IND enables organised criminal activity falsifying the discourse of corruption in the state sector.

The licit state agency by its operational process is enabling a sustainable illicit enterprise situated in the bowels of the licit state agency premised on a working alliance with transnational organised crime.

The data listed in the appendices of the audit report provide insights into the terrain of transnational organised crime that agents of the state in the illicit enterprise of the sale of state immigration and naturalisation documents navigate on a daily basis. It's readily apparent that agents and operations of Chinese transnational organised crime is the most widely listed reality of the appendices. The next is the major operational presence of Russian transnational organised crime. With the operations of the MTTOs being the masked hegemon of the illicit order. As all transnational organised crime groups operating within the bounds of this illicit enterprise are impacted by and have to recognise the hegemony of the MTTOs over the illicit trades of Belize. The MTTOs dominate the flow of persons into Belize from Latin America who are using Belize as a jump off point to Mexico whether they exit Belize in a short or longer time frame. Then there are those who enter Belize to work in the structure of the illicit trades of Belize including those in command and control positions. Then there are those who enter Belize seeking to establish hustles which require they engage with the state as legal entry is vitally necessary to open doors to ensure operational security. The snake heads of China sell their service packages for licit entry to Belize demanding payment in advance. Those who can only afford the budget/economy packages are the most liable to become targets of extortion where they become bonded to the snake heads to dispose of as they see fit. Those from China who are utilising family ties to a resident of Belize are still faced with the task of running the gauntlet of the snake heads and the Mexican Transnational Trafficking Organisations (MTTOs) ultimately to access the services of the illicit enterprise. Those seeking to bypass these gate keepers will then seek out agents of the state and politicians willing to offer their services. To do so places one in peril as the long reach of the arm of ethnic and race based transnational organised crime is soon felt. Those appendices which show persons resorting to fake legal documents for sponsors of applicants not only illustrate the activities of organised crime but more so of those seeking to run hustles in the illicit immigration business that must by pass and run parallel to the operational methodology of transnational crime. The reality is when a client purchased a premier package upon arrival in Belize there is a seamless transition to the granting of a visa which will not be picked up by the audit team. Those who paid for budget packages or choose to hire out independent service providers within the agency for a cut rate fee are predominantly those who made the appendices of the audit report. The cost of the service package purchased directly determines the quality of the product delivered. The difference between being named in an audit report and being a ghost in the apparatus of the agency. Are these successful applicants who they say they are on the applications lodged at the Belize IND? For the right price paid in US dollars no you are not!

The Chinese and the Latin Americans have always viewed Belize as a staging area in their strategy for illicit migrants to enter the US. What is now apparent from the audit report is the growing range of nationalities now traveling to

Belize for the same reason. Persons from South Asia, Africa and the Middle East are now in the mix and this is the result of the hegemony the MTTOs now exercise over human smuggling in the Caribbean basin. The depth and expanse of the operational activity of the Chinese snake heads in Belize indicate an operational presence that has evolved from the foundation the Triads laid during British colonial domination in Belize to the snake heads of the People's Republic of China today with smuggling links to the US and Canada laid under the Triads maintained to the present. But the snake heads have evolved the smuggling strategy to now include permanent settlement of Chinese in Belize where they work in snake head owned enterprises both licit and illicit and are moved around the Caribbean basin to work in snake head owned and controlled licit and illicit enterprises. The snake heads finance the front businesses which then receive and absorb the Chinese transported by the snake heads to the Caribbean. This movement then masks the parallel illicit enterprises which now have a dual flow structure with people and goods from China as synthetic drug precursors and fake goods. With illicit drugs, precious stones, gold, diamonds and animal organs as fish bladders etc. to China. The snake heads are now suppliers of Chinese sex workers to the Caribbean basin.

This methodology of the snake heads utilised for smuggling Chinese illicit migrants from the Peoples Republic of China is also operational particularly in Trinidad and Tobago, Guyana and Suriname as in Belize.

The salient questions that arises from the revelation of the audit report of the activities of the Russians in Belize are as follows: Is it a gateway as is the case with the Chinese, Latin Americans and others? Is Belize an operational base for money laundering and the acquisition of a nationality other than Russian? Is Belize one operational area amongst others in the Caribbean basin where Russian organised crime blends operationally with the MTTOs, their partners and affiliates? What is the nature of the organisational structure of Russian organised crime in Belize?

Analysis of the audit report raises the issue of the nature and functioning of the state in neo colonial social orders in the Caribbean basin premised on the Westminster model of government. With constitutional decolonisation/ independence these former British colonies inherited the expanse of contested spaces in the social order created by the British colonial state. Over time since independence the expanse and depth of these contested spaces have evolved, expanded and heightened because of the failure of the ruling elites to grasp the necessity of specific types of power relations in these states founded on the established constitutional model. Emphasis has been placed on sovereignty and law to the detriment of the necessary and compulsory task of discipline and domination premised on mechanisms of the nexus: power/knowledge. Failing to grasp the reality that power must be exercised or it's exercised upon you it's not a thing to be held, owned nor is it an entitlement. The ruling elite is mesmerised by the discourse of sovereignty which renders them monarchs with the prime minister being the prime monarch in their own minds. Mechanisms of power/knowledge must be unleashed towards the generation of discourse which drives the application of power in relations where discipline/domination is the strategic aim. The fixation with sovereignty generates the belief that a special group holds power by law and must not be challenged which obviates the need for exercising power/power relations throughout the social order as their power is a given even an absolute. This position has then driven the expanse and depth of contested spaces in the social order as it gives space to rebellious power/knowledge and their attendant discourses to challenge those who are under the delusion that power is an object they hold. Those addicted to sovereignty concentrate on general elections as the only relevant power struggle they are concerned with and with victory comes the spoils of dominating the state. This further enhances their refusal to grasp the need for engaging in the production of apparatuses and mechanisms of power with its attendant knowledge and discourse of truth towards disciplining and dominating the social order. But this failure has now resulted in general agencies of power as state institutions incapable of responding to threats to the state. For the general forms of power must be constantly renewed by the mechanisms created in response to power relations on the ground in the quest for discipline and domination. In these states the general agencies of power have fallen into stasis precipitating a crisis of sustainable survival of the state and its social order.

The ruling elites especially the politicians have responded to this crisis by insisting that the problem is state corruption. But they will never see much less publicly admit that the problem is the manner in which the ruling elite defines power and its operation within the context of the Westminster model of government. The prime driving force of the social order presumed under the Westminster model is the domination of the social order by power/knowledge and its power relations masked by the discourse of sovereignty and law. Where law and sovereignty serve and enables power/knowledge in its quest for discipline/domination. The ruling elites don't get the message as they are still trapped in a colonial worldview failing to understand that there was no Westminster model applied under the colonial order. This was the order of massa, smiles and blood and you simply cannot hope to replicate this colonial order today.

The independence experiment in the British Caribbean colonies was then premised on an attempt to graft unto a colonial order a mechanism of power that was not organic to that of the colonial order. In fact, the two mechanisms of power are diametrically opposed and the colonial order rejected the graft. The independence experiment is then in tatters as the ruling elite has created a state and its social order that is a Frankenstein monster, neither colonial nor Westminster. The state is not then corrupt it's malformed, undernourished, brain dead and non-sustainable exemplified by the chronic violence and the inability to change regardless of who rules in conjunction with the so-called inherent superiority of the oligarchs. Primarily the result of the addiction of the ruling elites to the discourse of sovereignty is seen where they insist that the primary issue is attacks on the state not the moribund operational nature of the general mechanisms of power of the state. For no one should avail themselves of the opportunity to assault the state and those who do can only do so via state corruption. A discourse that denies the history of the evolution of the power/knowledge state form from reason of state to biopolitics from whence the Westminster model came.

The discourse of corruption is then another product of the delusion of the ruling elite which addresses nothing and solves nothing for the problem is the ruling elite in the context of the organic demand of the Westminster model. Lumpen elite, lumpen state, violent social order.

References

"Special Audit-Visa Immigration and Nationality Department for the period 2011-2013" Office of the Auditor General of Belize

www.audit.gov.bz/downloads/Visa.pdf[1]

---

1. http://www.audit.gov.bz/downloads/Visa.pdf

CHAPTER 2
The Power Relations of the Alliance

In 2016 a Select Committee of the Senate of Belize was established to investigate through public sessions the report of the Auditor General of Belize on the Audit of the Immigration and Naturalisation Department (IND). This analysis will focus on the various discourses utilised by the persons who testified before the said Senate Committee. The senior management of the IND delivered a specific discourse, the politicians who appeared delivered their own specific discourse, the non- managerial staff of the IND delivered multiple discourses namely: the discourse of being powerless when faced with political demands, the discourse of the whistle blower and the discourse of innocence. There was the discourse of those not employed at the IND but were agents of the state which is the discourse of faithfully executing assigned duties in a most difficult operational terrain. And there was the discourse of a participant of the organised crime enterprise.

What is most noteworthy in the accounts of the public sessions published in the Belizean press is the use of the discourse of corruption by the senior managers and the line staff of the IND appearing at the Senate Committee. The discourse of the politicians at the hearings of the Senate Committee evaded using the discourse of corruption.

The Public Servants before the Senate Committee

In January 2017 when the public hearings of the Senate Committee commenced the testimony of Ruth Meighan former Immigration Director to the Senate Committee was reported in the press. Meighan in her testimony unleashed a discourse of self-exoneration which refused to utilise the discourse of corruption. Meighan states: "There is a culture at the immigration department; I don't know about a scheme because I practically gave approval to those things on the understanding that the information that was presented to me was accurate information, so all the approval that I gave was given on the information that was presented." Meighan at the apex of the hierarchy of the Immigration Department cannot be blamed for approving 12 permanent residency applications for applicants who didn't qualify as her decisions are as good as the information forwarded to her. There is then no oversight and the apex of the pyramid is deaf, dumb and blind even brain dead. The impunity of ignorance. On her second appearance at the Committee hearings Megan insisted that Belizean passports could have been issued during the period in which she was the Director without her knowledge and approval bearing her signature. Meighan states: "At the time I became Director, I was asked to put my signature on the passport system, which is the approved signature for passports, but in terms of my intervention in the process from application up to that point, after signing on that system, I have absolutely no intervention in that process, from application up to the time of approval. My signature is on a passport system that approves the passport." Again the discourse of the impunity of ignorance. Meighan then names the official with the power she says she didn't have as Director namely: the officer in charge of the passport section. But in the power relations of the IND the said officer formally reports to Meighan. Meighan indicated her position on approvals given to applicants recommended by Ministers of Government as follows: "The applications were processed and approved by my desk even with the Minister's recommendation based on the information that is presented to me by the officer saying that the person meets the requirements for the visas." Visas approved for unworthy applicants recommended by ministers are not the fault of Meighan or the ministers but solely that of the officer who informed Meighan to the contrary. Meighan stated her position on ministers visiting the IND as follows: "If the Minister came to the office to see me, then I see them, if they are there for any other business and they didn't come to my office, I asked no question about what they are doing there." "and I am saying, if the Minister is there, like everybody else, they are entitled to visit any of the offices, any of the government offices." This is the discourse of the hegemony of ruling politicians over agents and organs of the state which is a mask for the power relations of the apparatus contrived to exert the hegemony of ruling politicians over the agents and organs of the state. Meighan is then lucid in her position of affirming the hegemony of ruling politicians over her when she was the Director of Immigration.

Meighan has indicated in her testimony that the mandate of the Immigration department is defined by the hegemony of the ruling politicians which results in the operational reality of the department that the security of Belize entrusted to the department is determined by the imperatives of the ruling politicians. Ruling politicians bent on their agendas which compromise the security of Belize will not be hindered in their drive by the director of the department. Which in turn means that any politically connected officer of the department attesting to the veracity of an application or applications will have those applications approved by the director. For Meighan there is no culture of corruption in the department what there is a department that exists to serve ruling politicians. The outcome of this subservience to ruling politicians is the soul of impunity that envelops the actions of the foot-soldiers of the politicians in the department. What actions have been taken to prosecute the perpetrators of illegal acts uncovered in the report of the Auditor-General? This enables Meighan's discourse of self-exoneration released at the hearings of the Senate Committee by pleading powerlessness in office. A contradiction in terms.

The People's United Party (PUP) lost the 2012 general elections to the United Democratic Party (UDP) by 812 votes. In the aftermath of this narrow loss the PUP has insisted that the UDP utilised the Immigration and Naturalisation Department in the run up to the 2012 elections to grant nationality illicitly to applicants who then registered to vote in the 2012 general elections. The current leader of the PUP, John Briceno, in the House of Representatives in December 2016 as reported in Amandala.com stated as follows on this issue: "I was given 64 pages of, names of people who got their nationality, between October 2011 and February 2012. Over 2,000 nationalities were issued just before the election. Here we have the names." On January 26, 2017 Ruth Meighan was questioned on the role of the Immigration and Naturalisation department in this political issue by PUP Senator Eamon Courtney. In response to Courtney's questions Meighan states: "I am aware that Ministers were trying to get people processed for nationality during that period." Meighan says yes that it was on an expedited basis that the department was processing applications for nationality. Meighan says yes to the position that applications for nationality were being expedited in order for recipients to be registered to vote in the upcoming general election of 2012. In response to the questions posed dealing with incomplete applications of persons who were granted nationality which meant they received Belizean nationality illicitly and voted illicitly in the 2012 general elections. Meighan responded as follows: "Those persons did not qualify, but the files were presented, and I could clearly remember my Minister coming back and telling me...because we were concerned about the files, they were requesting a lot of files, and we said that we have to ensure that all the applicants meet the requirements for nationality, and that was clearly stated throughout the department, and so, any files that came to us for approval, they were presented as qualified applicants." Meighan is then insisting that the illicit process was driven by the ruling UDP politicians and the IND simply complied and facilitated the illicit process. For Meighan the granting of illicit nationality in the run up to the 2012 general elections was the most potent indication of the hegemony of ruling politicians over the IND with the complicity of the agents of the state posted at the IND. Meighan said yes there were fraudulent successful applications. Yes, these applicants didn't qualify for nationality and to register to vote. Meighan posits to the Senate Committee the position of the PUP is then highly probable.

http://amandala.com.bz/news/ruth-meighan-knows-nothing-immigration-dept-scandal/

http://amandala.com.bz/news/ruth-meighans-electronic-signature-immigration-system/

http://amandala.com.bz/news/ruth-meighan-didnt-didnt-care-ministers-immigration-visits/

http://amandala.com.bz/news/immigration-free-for-all/

Maria Marin former Director of the Immigration Department and Deputy Director during the period of the audit when Ruth Meighan was the Director testified before the Senate Committee. Marin unleashed the discourse of rightful duty in her testimony by insisting she did her duty by: attempting to tackle the culture of irregularities in the IND when she was Director. During her tenure of Deputy Director, she refused to comply with the culture of accepting and approving incomplete applications in the IND. She then wrote reports on glaring irregularities in the operations of the IND passing those reports to the Minister with responsibility for the IND. Those reports also laid charges against specific employees of the IND who were involved with said irregularities. Marin also stated that in response to the Ministerial influence over the department in the issuance of visas, permanent residence, nationality and passports she prepared a list of applications bearing Ministers as recommenders and sent said list to the Minister with responsibility for the IND. Marin executed her rightful duty which meant that the failure to change the culture of the IND was the result of political indifference as it served the political agenda for the IND in the period and thereafter. Marin states in her testimony that after becoming Director of the IND the culture persisted. Marin is insisting that the culture of irregularities at the IND is the product of the power relations between the IND and the ruling politicians of the day where the ruling politicians are exerting hegemony over the IND. In her presentation Marin names an employee of the IND as a person of special interest in the culture of indifference to the IND by those in authority: Ady Pacheco. It was also revealed that Marin wrote reports as Deputy Director on two cases of the illicit granting of nationality and passports by the IND: the case of Won Hong Kim and the case of David Nanes Schnitzer. Both cases potently indicate the operations of transnational organised crime in conjunction with the ruling politicians of Belize and the employees of the IND.

The case of David Nanes

David Nanes was a fugitive from Mexican justice wanted for being part of the Allen Stanford Ponzi scheme in Mexico residing in Belize. In a memo dated December 11, 2015 by the then Director of Immigration, Maria Marin, to the then CEO of the Ministry of Immigration, Edward Zuniga, Marin detailed the process by which Nanes obtained Belizean nationality by fraudulent means. On November 29, 2012 David Nanes applied for Belizean nationality using the name David Banes. On the affidavit supplied with the application and on the references provided by two referees the name of the applicant was David Nanes not David Banes and Ady Pacheco of the IND issued a nationality Passport Receipt in the name of David Nanes not David Banes the applicants name. All the supporting documents submitted with the application of David Banes were issued for David Nanes including a police report, a medical examination, a marriage certificate and a Bank of America statement. Ady Pacheco collected the fees from Nanes and issued a receipt for David Banes. Both the Officer in Charge of the Nationality Section and the Director approved Nanes'/Banes' application for Belizean nationality. The photocopy of the US passport submitted by Banes was subsequently found to be fraudulent as the surname in the passport was Banes but in the machine readable zone of the passport the surname was Nanes. The US Embassy to Belize when contacted reported that the said passport was issued on January 14, 2008 in Miami, Florida to David M Nanes not Banes. The Embassy stated that the US passport used by Banes with his application bore "readily apparent fraudulent indicators." Pacheco signed the copy of the passport validating it as a true copy of Banes' US passport, the Officer in Charge approved the process and the Director signed off on it. Pacheco personally handled the entire Banes process from receiving the application to completing the process within a record 19 days. Pacheco stated that Banes was a permanent residence holder from 2004, then changed the date to 2006 and stated that he was married in Belize on the relevant forms. But there was no Belizean marriage certificate to support this claim nor a permanent resident permit. The permit number of the permanent residency stamp in his passport was issued to one Warren Edward Mudry. Banes did not sign an oath nor attend the swearing in ceremony for successful applicants for Belizean nationality compulsory under law. Banes was issued his certificate of Belizean nationality illicitly by persons within the IND and the Ministry of Immigration. Banes with the nationality certificate then obtained all existing identity documents of Belize as a passport. This case was not part of the audit report therefore outside of the remit of the Senate Committee. In November 2015 Banes a resident of San Pedro, Belize was arrested and charged for being in possession of fraudulent documents, granted bail in spite of his flight risk and the knowledge that he was a fugitive from Mexican justice and simply disappeared. Banes/Nanes was arrested in Mexico in 2017 when he returned to Mexico aboard a flight from Cuba with a new identity in tow. Such is the long arm of the MTTOs.

The Banes/Nanes case provides insights into the transnational organised crime enterprise within the IND and the Ministry of Immigration in Belize. An enterprise driven by an alliance with the ruling politicians and the public servants of the IND and the Ministry. Illustrated by the level of impunity enjoyed by those operatives of this illicit enterprise employed at the IND. What is noteworthy is the operational sophistication of the illicit enterprise within the IND as Marin was alerted to the Nanes case by a police officer following the arrest of Nanes in San Pedro and the audit report contained no mention of it much less details of it. This reality indicates that within the IND methods are utilised which effectively mask the illicit access to IND documents when it's so required and necessary from discovery after the event for a price. This service is especially prized by Transnational Criminal Organisations (TCOs). How many TCOs' traffickers are there in the Caribbean basin and Europe in possession of valid Belizean passports?

http://amandala.com.bz/news/ministerial-influence-ruled-immigration-department/

http://www.reporter.bz/general/schnitzer-was-facilitated-just-like-kim-wong-hong-documents-show/

http://amandala.com.bz/news/hustle-david-nanesbanes-schnitzers-nationality-documents/

In November 2017 Marin made her second appearance before the Senate Committee. In her second appearance Marin read from a prepared statement and stated in 2013 the substantive Minister of Immigration Godwin Hulse told her that: "a specific process was to be followed for those visa applications recommended/supported by Government Ministers." "After much discussion, the following was decided: All applications supported by Ministers/caretakers would come to the Ministry for initial vetting. The Ministry will then hand over to the Director of Immigration under confidential cover. Ministers or caretakers shall not act as agents or sponsors, but simply as support for the applicant or sponsor." But it's clear from her testimony to the Committee Marin complied with the application process even though she was of the position that it breached the procedures of the IND. Marin insists that she was an agent for change in the department but was stymied by the lack of support from the Ministry and its Minister and CEO. But admits that she was unable to command the disciplined support of key officers of the department as they openly refused to adhere to her directives. Marin spoke of the open flaunting by officers in the department of their influence with her superiors political or otherwise. Marin joined the IND in April 2009 as Deputy Director, in February 2013 she became Director and in April 2016 she was transferred from the IND without any reason being given. She stated that in 2016 whilst still in the IND she was notified that she was demoted to Deputy Director. Marin insists that these are instances of the persecution she experienced being an agent for change at the IND in her testimony driven by the discourse of rightful duty and victimhood derived from thereof. Within this discourse there are no revelations of the organised crime enterprise described in the audit report of the IND. Marin is so focused on retrieving and reconstructing her concept of her public image that she refuses to deal with the substantive issue of the audit report: organised crime at the IND during her tenure as Deputy Director and Director of the IND. Marin reveals the special process to handle applications for visas recommended by Ministers of government, insists that it was a breach of procedure of the IND yet insists to the Committee that all of the proper checks and investigations were carried out by the IND under her charge. Where then did the breaches reported in the audit come from?

This operational reality common to public servants who appeared before the Senate Committee shines light on the reality that in the apparatuses of power of the power relations between ruling politicians, public servants and organised crime public servants adopt the operational strategies of non-elected politicians. Thereby further politicising the public service and agencies of the state as it's an instrument in the force/power relations and the ceaseless struggles derived thereof between politicians, public servants and organised crime under the Westminster model as that of Belize.

http://www.reporter.bz/front-page/nothing-but-the-truth-marin-takes-the-stand-again/

http://amandala.com.bz/news/yu-gaan-rock-di-hustling-boat-maria/

http://amandala.com.bz/news/maria-marin-immigration-ministry-instructed-officers-abandon-full-vetting-expedite-visa-applications-recommended-ministers-caretakers/

Teresita Castellanos testified before the Senate Committee reading from a prepared text. During the period of the audit carried out by the office of the Auditor General Castellanos was the Finance Officer of the Immigration Department until her transfer in 2014. Castellanos utilised a dual discourse during her testimony comprising the discourse of endemic corruption and the discourse of rightful duty. Using the discourse of endemic corruption Castellanos states: "I was in the belly of the beast for three years and am among others named in the Auditor General's Report. This gives me the right to say the following." "The Immigration Department has an entrenched culture of corruption and hustling...milking the cow, as we say from the very top to the very bottom of the ladder. No politician can force any public officer to do illegal acts when performing our jobs. And if we do, then we have to face the same consequences as the politicians," Castellanos continues: "There are a few good, honest and dedicated officers, but there were not enough trusted staff to oversee the daily operations of the sections and the district offices and the border stations. The call for help was not answered, and this inquiry is the result." The discourse of rightful duty was used as follows: "The Department, headed by the Acting Director and her small team, made many attempts to stop the rampant malpractices that plagued the Department. The job to fix the problem was too difficult to accomplish, the reason being was the often non-support from our Ministry. We considered ourselves orphans of the Ministry." "The resistance to follow orders given by the Head of Department and to adhere to the Government regulations was frustrating." "I would like to go further and state that the resistance by some officers was beyond my comprehension. At one point some of us were fearful for the life of Acting Director Maria Marin. Why? Because she was doing her job, she was strict, because she was putting things in place for the hustling to stop." Castellanos is insisting that the staff of the Immigration department is corrupt to the core aided and abetted by the ruling politicians of the day. The ruling politicians had the opportunity to recreate the department through the leadership of Maria Marin and her small dedicated team which included Castellanos but refused to do so. Therefore, an endemically corrupt department of immigration serves the interests of the ruling politicians of the day. For daring to stand for integrity and the rule of law Castellanos was removed from the department.

The dual discourse of Castellanos unleashed at the Senate Committee hearings complemented and expanded upon that utilised by Maria Marin at the hearings of the said committee. Castellanos ventured where Marin chose not to go with the discourse of corruption and made Marin the exemplary leader in her discourse of rightful duty. The objective was to present Castellanos as a victim of an endemically corrupt department in the service of the ruling politicians. The assault of the discourse is on the ruling politicians as the source of the evil which by extension presents the plight of the public officer intent on rightful duty in a state agency under the hegemony of the ruling politicians.

http://amandala.com.bz/news/corrupt-top-bottom/

Therese Chavarria testified before the Senate Committee in her then capacity of immigration officer during the period of the audit of the IND. Chavarria now retired at her Senate Committee hearing unleashed the discourse of the whistle blower from within the IND by revealing the case of the illicit application for a passport that was granted on the instructions of a Cabinet Minister. The applicant according to Chavarria was a minor accompanied by a Justice of the Peace/translator with a Chinese name as the applicant. When questioned the applicant failed to answer relevant questions as to his daily life in Belize in spite of the fact that a Belizean birth certificate for the applicant was submitted with the application. Chavarria subsequently rejected the application and held on to it for investigation which she commenced by contacting the Principal of the school the applicant was reportedly a student of. Chavarria proceeded on leave with the application in her possession to learn from the then Director Meighan that during her absence the JP/translator submitted a new application for the individual and a Cabinet Minister instructed that a Belizean passport be issued and it was so done. Chavarria also indicated that she briefed the Auditor General on this issue. The discourse is in fact describing an organised crime operation with illicit demand being satisfied by illicit supply via the deliberate action of ruling politicians and complicit agents of the state. But it relentlessly insists that the ruling politicians are the kingpins which is an attempt to mask the actions of the public servants/ agents of the state which Castellanos describes as "hustling" making them multiple identity/action agents where they execute the instructions of the kingpins and run independent and joint hustles of their own as public servants/agents of the state enabled by the impunity service to the kingpins affords them. An online news report dated September 27, 2013 in reporter.bz stated as follows: "Penner, however, has not been the only immigration ministerial casualty. During the first term of the Dean Barrow led UDP government, Carlos Perdomo lost the immigration portfolio, after numerous scandals involving the granting of Belize visas and passports from the Belize embassy in Havana to Asians who were landing by the plane loads at the Philip Goldson International Airport." Carlos Perdomo is the minister named by Chavarria in her testimony.

http://amandala.com.bz/news/carlos-perdomos-called-reference-shady-issuance-passport/

http://www.reporter.bz/front-page/penner-should-face-criminal-charges-says-psu-presdient/

Revelations from within an organised crime ring

Alvarine Burgess in her testimony to the Senate Committee provided descriptions and insights into the operational practices of the organised crime enterprise that sold licit Belize visas to illicit applicants. Burgess was a courier charged with the tasks of transporting the B$ 2,000 per visa application charged by the Minister named by Burgess as Edmond Castro, the visa applications and the native passports of the visa applicants. Burgess was also charged with transporting the native passports of the applicants to the immigration department, then collect the official receipts and pass them to the police officer who interfaced with the clients. For her duties Burgess received B$ 1,500 per trip to the immigration department. Burgess stated that in the absence of Castro she acquired the service of two other Ministers. Burgess states that Castro demanded payment in advance for his visa service plus the possession of the passport of the visa applicant which he passed to Burgess for transportation to the immigration department and lodging them plus their retrieval. Castro handled the transportation to and lodging of the visa applications in the immigration department. Burgess describes an organised crime ring encased in impunity as the named Ministers cared very little about plausible denial. The discourse of corruption simply cannot explain the operational realities of this organised crime enterprise with its links to transnational organised crime especially the snake heads. There is then a network of operatives in the immigration department and other state agencies as the police who willingly participate for their personal benefit and gain embellished by career advancement within the state agencies. Burgess stated that she was interviewed by US officials who played back for her a recordings of a conversation involving Castro. This indicated the interest of agencies of the US federal state in the issues raised by the revelations of the various IND scandals. Burgess was sued by Castro for defamation in 2015 but he subsequently withdrew his legal action before its completion.

Burgess' testimony gave an insight into an organised crime ring that was driven by the sale of services by government ministers. It affords little insights into the power relations between government ministers and employees of the IND. And none at all into the operational nature of employees of the IND involved in their own organised crime enterprises with transnational organised crime to the exclusion of government ministers. The strategy is to point fingers at government Ministers thereby politicising the engagement with the IND in an attempt to preserve the operational capacity of existing organised crime enterprises in the IND and to ensure impunity for all participants. The expectation is that demand for services will grow and the ruling politicians will not cease and desist from selling the services of the IND.

http://amandala.com.bz/news/finally-ministers-named/

http://www.reporter.bz/front-page/alvarine-burgess-provides-explosive-testimony/

Public Servants before the Committee

Mark Tench employee of the IND in his testimony to the Senate Committee dealt with his discovery of the missing 8 visa stickers at the Belize West Border Station (BWBS) and the investigation he subsequently did into the disappearance. Tench discovered the 8 missing visa stickers in the stock of visa stickers on hand with no record of their disposal in the official record. Tench alerted the two other immigration officers on the shift with Tench and his superior at the BWBS Edgar Cano as to the missing 8 visa stickers. Tench continued investigating the case of the stolen visa stickers which led him to Patrick Tillett, former financial controller of the Belize City Council. Tench arranged a meeting with Tillett in Belize City but at this meeting between Tench, two other immigration officers and Tillett Eric Chang was present, former Deputy Mayor of the Belize City Council. On the meeting with Chang and Tillett, Tench states as follows: "Mr. Chang informed us he was the one who was getting the visas for some people and they had bought it through a person and they had realised that the visas were not good, not valid and that is why they had taken it to Belmopan office. What they wanted, they wanted us to help them get back their money, that was why they chose to meet with us." Tench continues: "They admitted they had bought the visas. They paid $5,000 per visa, and the visas were not done properly. Tench stated that Chang and Tillett indicated that they purchased the visas from a Mr Middleton who said that he got the visas from one Gaddafi from Corozal. Tench told the Committee that he interviewed Gaddafi who described Mr Middleton as the brains of the operation. Tench testified to the Committee that on his return from interviewing Gaddafi in Corozal he indicated to Edgar Cano that at this juncture of the investigation the police must be called in to the investigation which Cano never did. How did Chang and Tillett expect Tench and the other immigration officers to recover the money paid for the stolen visas? Did Chang and Tillett seek to utilise the Belmopan office to have the 8 stolen visas legally issued to their clients? By formally reporting the 8 visas missing and then pursuing an investigation Tench threw a spanner in the works of the organised crime enterprise. To expect the Belmopan office of the IND to issue the stolen 8 visas as legal visas illustrates the level of impunity that pervades the system. To do so in the face of the report of the 8 stolen visas and an ongoing investigation is an expectation that threatens the sustainability of the organised crime enterprise. Tench in his testimony insists that an employee of the BWBS was most likely the culprit in the theft of the visas an inside job then but he calls no name. Tench describes the damage control the management of the IND then undertook to restore some semblance of legality whilst maintain the state of endemic impunity within the IND. Tench and another employee of the IND had formal disciplinary charges laid against them for the disappearance of the 8 visas. No criminal investigation leading to criminal charges against Tench was done. Tench was exonerated of the charges by the Public Service Commission (PSC) according to the correspondence from the PSC he provided to the Committee. In her testimony to the Committee former CEO of Immigration Candelaria Saldivar-Morter stated that the PSC sanctioned Tench for the missing 8 visas and charged him $16,000.

In his testimony before the Senate Committee Tillett admitted to: having in his possession six of the illicit visa foils for six clients of his desirous of obtaining Belize visas, the conspiracy with Eric Chang and the use of Mr Middleton as a facilitator of the conspiracy.

http://amandala.com.bz/news/so-stole-8-visa-stickers-immigration-department/

http://www.reporter.bz/business/senior-officer-exposes-cover-up-at-immigration/

http://www.reporter.bz/front-page/chang-and-tillett-finally-take-the-stand/

Inez Cassanova an employee of the IND in her testimony before the Senate Committee revealed the identity of Mr Middleton. IND employee Vernon Leslie in his report on the stolen 8 visa foils insisted that it was Leslie Wade who removed the 8 visa foils and handed them over to Mr Middleton who is the common law husband of Inez Cassanova. Cassanova in her testimony countered by insisting that Eugene Middleton was a former employee of the IND who worked with her at the Orange Walk Immigration office and through Eugene she knew his brother Barton Middleton. The Senate Committee summoned Barton Middleton to appear before the Committee and in his testimony he denied all the statements made by witnesses before the Committee concerning his involvement in the conspiracy to steal and sell 8 Belize visas. Barton Middleton in fact in keeping with the operational rules of transnational organised crime abided by the iron law of silence indicating his fear for his life and invoking his right to silence.

http://amandala.com.bz/news/mysterious-mr-middleton-unmasked-cassanova/

http://www.reporter.bz/front-page/mr-middleton-scared-for-life-but-cant-recall/

http://amandala.com.bz/news/horrible-terrible-memory-barton-middleton/

http://www.reporter.bz/front-page/nothing-more-to-say-middleton-tells-senate/

http://amandala.com.bz/news/barton-middleton-invokes-constitutional-shut-up/

Police Inspector Rochelle Chan named by Alvarine Burgess in her testimony to the Committee appeared before the Senate Committee. Chan in his testimony denied all the claims made by Burgess saying they were lies, questioned the mental stability and competence of Burgess and made reference to an agenda by unnamed persons in the shadows using Burgess as an instrument. Chan utilised the discourse of attacking the credibility of the witness, of conspiracy theory and most of all his victimhood in the face of his innocence and impeccable record as a police officer.

http://www.reporter.bz/front-page/chan-takes-the-stand-perdomo-reappears-before-senate/

Ady Pacheco an employee of the IND named in connection with the Wong Hong Kim case for having received and accepted an incomplete application form for Belizean nationality and a passport from Wong Hong Kim. Wong Hong Kim was a national of South Korea detained in a Taiwanese jail on a South Korean arrest warrant when a nationality certificate of Belize and a Belizean passport were issued for Kim fraudulently. The report of the audit of the IND named Pacheco as the IND employee who received the incomplete Kim application and acted upon it. Pacheco in her testimony stated that she received the incomplete Kim application in the presence of her IND supervisor Gordon Wade from then Minister of State in the Ministry of Immigration Elvin Penner. Pacheco stated that Penner promised to provide the missing documents and the incomplete application was accepted though no official receipt for it was issued as it was incomplete. Pacheco didn't see Kim in the IND and she made no inquiry as to his whereabouts. Pacheco indicated that it was nothing unusual to accept and act upon incomplete applications at the IND on this Pacheco stated: "it was nothing out of the ordinary at the time. Up to now I think there are still hundreds of files that are incomplete." Pacheco testified that incomplete applications came to Wade from Cabinet Ministers, their drivers and secretaries who would instruct her to accept and process them. Other incomplete applications were only accepted and processed by Pacheco with Wade's permission. Pacheco gave as her reason for accepting and processing incomplete applications from ruling politicians fear of the power wielded by them and the politically connected. Pacheco states: "This is Belize, this is how it works, sadly, but it's the truth. If an officer does not comply with the request made by a minister, they simply move you to somewhere else."

Pacheco in her testimony utilises the dual discourse of political corruption and duress where the ruling politicians with the complicity of members of the IND are demanding compliance with illicit acts. Pacheco faced with this reality at the IND has no choice but to comply given the power the ruling politicians wield over her employment and by extension career advancement. Pacheco is the victim rather than the willing participant in an organised crime enterprise.

In her final appearance before the Senate Committee Pacheco was questioned about the theft from the Belmopan office of the IND of some 200 passport blanks in 2005 some of which were assigned to her. One of the stolen blanks was subsequently issued to a Chinese national in November 2007. Pacheco said the blanks arrived at the office on a Friday were stored in a desk drawer in the Passport office and discovered missing on the following Monday. In 2006 100 passport blanks were stolen. In both instances no criminal charges were laid. Potent instances of the impunity that drives the extent, depth, profitability and sustainability of this transnational organised crime enterprise in Belize. Ady Pacheco in her final appearance before the Senate Committee was questioned on the granting of a nationality certificate to a member of the Harmouch family in 2012 even though he didn't qualify for Belizean nationality as revealed in the audit report of the IND. The Officer in Charge of the Nationality

Section of the IND refused to recommend the applicant from the Harmouch family but a clerk of the nationality section did so recommend the applicant to the Director of Immigration who approved the application. The Harmouch nationality certificate was then signed by Elvin Penner. The audit report revealed that another member of the Harmouch family in 2005 was not recommended for a nationality certificate by the IND but was granted Belizean nationality by the then PUP government. What is noteworthy here is the Officer in Charge of the section refuses to recommend the applicant being by passed by a junior officer whose recommendation is accepted by the Director of Immigration even though this junior officer has no power to so do. This is facilitation of an illicit process which effectively rips apart the hierarchy of the agency of the public service which opens up the structure to effective domination by the ruling politicians, transnational crime and their minions in the structure.

http://amandala.com.bz/news/ady-pacheco-wont-respond-senate-select-committees-questions-lawyer/

http://amandala.com.bz/news/ady-pacheco-citizen-kim/

http://amandala.com.bz/news/200-passports-stolen-2005/

Edmund Zuniga Chief Executive Officer (CEO) in the Ministry of Immigration in his testimony before the Senate Committee stated as follows on the Auditor General's report on the IND: "We've reviewed the reports with that in mind. I would say that at this point in time, some of the actions that can be taken were already taken. There were public officers in the Immigration Department who were taken before the Public Services Commission. But of course, we all know the outcome of those meetings with the Public Services Commission." The Ministry of Immigration has then responded to the report in keeping with what is permissible under the rules and regulations governing the public service under the Westminster model of Belize's constitution. The issue of effectiveness is a matter that has to be raised at the political level which is outside the realm of the public service. Zuniga continues as follows: "When an Auditor General's report is completed and there are issues of fraud and theft or whatever, these reports are copied to the Commissioner of Police and the

Director of Public Prosecutions for them to start doing their own part of the investigation." "real investigation for fraud is a matter for the law enforcement agencies." The law enforcement agencies and the office of the Director of Public Prosecutions (DPP) are then charged with the task of investigating and prosecuting those responsible for illicit acts uncovered in the audit report of the IND under the constitution of Belize not the public service. Zuniga states: "It is up to the Commissioner of Police to instruct or to take on investigations without prompting from anybody." Zuniga is then calling out the Commissioner of Police (CoP) as the task of policing illegalities in the public service is the mandate of the CoP and the DPP. The question then is what is the CoP doing in response to the audit report on the IND by the office of the Auditor General?

http://amandala.com.bz/news/ceo-zuniga-blames-police-inaction-senate-inquiry-revelations/

Commissioner of Police (CoP) Allen Whylie testified before the Senate Committee before Edward Zuniga did. The Senate Committee questioned the CoP on three primary areas of interest: the investigation into the case of Wong Hong Kim, the public statement made by retired Superintendent of Police Julio Valdez on the termination of his investigation into immigration files removed illicitly from the IND and the course of action taken by the CoP in response to the audit report on the IND.

On the first primary area of interest the CoP indicated that the investigation into the matter of Wong Hong Kim the Belizean nationality and passport issued to Kim and the role of Elvin Penner in this matter was completed. On the second primary interest the CoP stated as follows in reference to Valdez: "He came in and provided with me with a verbal briefing in terms of the investigation. The impression I got was that perhaps he was running into some roadblocks at the Immigration Department and I reminded him that as police, we do have a responsibility to investigate and that he needed to get into the Immigration Department and see all those files and that if I needed to sign a search warrant for him to do that, I was prepared to do so." The CoP indicated that he received no final report from Valdez nor did he ever ask Valdez why there was no final report. The CoP justified his strategy as follows: "because the fact that there was an issue in the media that someone had told him, or stopped him from investigating-and I wanted to know who had, because I knew I hadn't." CoP Whylie gave his full support to the investigation of the IND being undertaken by Superintendent Valdez. Valdez never briefed the CoP on the nature of the warning to Valdez on pursuing the investigation and the reason for Valdez no longer pursuing said investigation. The CoP learned of the warning to Valdez and his reaction to it concerning the pursuit of the investigation via the media not from Valdez. In light of this the CoP is of the opinion that Valdez is still under orders to pursue the investigation as the CoP did not order Valdez to end the investigation. The discourse utilised by the CoP then reveals another line with a different objective. This line states that the CoP defined two paths to be pursued in the investigation of the IND by Valdez: the illicit removal of files from the IND and how they ended up in the possession of Saldivar and the investigation of irregularities contained in the recovered files and instructed Valdez to pursue the investigation of both paths. Valdez in testimony to the Committee stated that he was told by the unnamed person to pursue an investigation of only the disappearance of the IND files and how they ended up in the possession of Saldivar. Whylie states: "but what I am saying is that I cannot, up to today's date, understand how he could believe it was otherwise, because as I said, the conversation was done in the presence of another senior officer." Valdez at minimum misunderstood Whylie or at worse is using Whylie as the scapegoat for his refusal to complete the investigation as instructed by Whylie.

The CoP Whylie in his testimony before the Committee unleashed the dual discourse of rightful duty and dereliction of duty. The CoP insists in reference to the Valdez investigation he did everything called for by rightful duty to ensure a full and proper investigation was carried out into all aspects of the criminal action. The refusal of Valdez to complete the investigation as directed by the CoP amounts to dereliction of duty by Valdez. The objective is to discredit Valdez and by extension his message.

On the third primary interest the CoP testified that he had taken no action in response to the audit report on the IND meaning no ongoing investigations into matters raised in the audit report have been set in train as to the date (July

19, 2017) of his testimony to the Committee by the police. Whylie said that he did not receive a copy off the audit report from the Auditor General and since receiving a copy he has been going through the report. In addition, he will await the publication of the report of the proceedings of the Senate Committee before acting on the recommendations of the audit report.

Given the length of time that has elapsed between the date the crimes were committed and the commencement of investigations the question of the ability to collect prosecutable evidence arises as the perpetrators have had enough time to eliminate trails of evidence and to silence witnesses utilising various methodologies.

http://www.reporter.bz/front-page/compol-answers-to-senate-committee/

http://amandala.com.bz/news/compol-whylie-did-nothing-glaring-evidence-wrongdoing-immigration-department/

On July 19, 2017 retired Police Superintendent Julio Valdez appeared before the Senate Committee. The primary issue was his investigation into the IND files that were in the possession of Arthur Saldivar who subsequently handed the said files over to the police in October 2013. The police then decided to investigate the possession of IND files by Saldivar and the then head of National Crime Investigation, Russell Blackett assigned the task of investigation to Julio Valdez. Valdez indicated that in the course of the investigation into the removal of the files from the IND and the possession of said files by Saldivar he found discrepancies and irregularities in documents contained within the files. In response to these irregularities he then commenced an investigation into these documents with irregularities including the applicants who submitted said documents to the IND. Valdez indicated that the files in the possession of Saldivar passed through the hands of Ady Pacheco at the IND. In his testimony before the Committee Valdez states: "To date, I do not know or did not discover how those documents left the immigration office. My experience as a police officer, I saw that some of these did not coincide with people who come into the country and are granted nationality, so I commenced an investigation into the Nationality section, the application itself." Valdez continues: "I was already following the Immigration and Nationality Section and based on what I already encountered, I was waiting for the audit, and I had already visited all other addresses I did not follow up that because the main concern was that I should follow up the missing documents out of the Immigration department." "The instructions were, deal with the investigations over the missing documents. Based on that, I did not continue the other line of investigation." When asked by the Committee to identify who ordered Valdez to cease from investigating irregularities of the application forms of the documents illicitly removed from the IND Valdez refused to answer the question citing "legal ramifications". When asked it was a member of the police Valdez refused to answer. When asked if he received instructions from outside the police Valdez states: "There were no instructions". Valdez is therefore indicating that the order to cease and desist from investigating the irregularities of the application forms was issued by a member of the police with the rank to so do to Valdez. Valdez indicated that he was not willing to name the person who gave him the order for to do so will result in him being involved in a legal battle to prove the accuracy of his statement and he wanted no part of that as he was now retired. Valdez wrote a report to the DPP on what his investigations revealed and stated that he was ordered to cease his investigation into the irregularities of application forms in the documents handed to police by Saldivar. Valdez stated in his testimony to the Committee that certain application forms bore addresses where the applicants were not residing at, some addresses were empty lots and some were totally fictitious with street names that don't exist.

http://amandala.com.bz/news/valdez-refused-call-name/

http://www.reporter.bz/front-page/compol-answers-to-senate-committee/

Valdez in his testimony to the Committee utilised the discourse of rightful duty emphasising the reality that power confines, limits and abrogates rightful duty even though rightful duty is grounded in sovereignty and law.

The power/force relations that enmesh public servants in Belize are then masked by the discourse of rightful duty hence sovereignty and law illustrating that this discourse is subservient to power/force relations. There are then as revealed in the testimonies before the Committee presented here two spheres of power relations: the internal power relations of the departments between public servants and the power relations between public servants and the ruling politicians. The ruling politicians exert hegemony over the public servants, the discourse of rightful duty, sovereignty and law. The nature of this hegemony in its operational reality doesn't fit into the Westminster system of government nor does it fit into the colonial imperial planation mode. It is in fact a hybrid of both the colonial, imperial mode and the Westminster model which is in effect a model of government where politics and its nature overdetermines the social order. Where political power relentlessly seeks to penetrate and determine the nature of all spaces and the power relations therein in the social order. Political power is then addicted to seeking to dominate and define all power relations in all spaces of the social order as political of the grand order. The discourse of corruption cannot locate and disentangle the power relations of this Frankenstein monster which accounts for its inability to explain the institutional inertia even stasis of these social orders since the commencement of the independence experiment. This also applies to the discourse of failed states as both discourses and their attendant worldviews cannot see the reality that all the signs of being shitholes a la Trump are organic products of the power relations of the social order which is a product of history. And there are powerful international power relations that ensure that we continue to embrace the legacies of history that constitute this Frankenstein monster. The power relations of these shitholes are functioning as designed, in keeping with their capacity and capability throwing up a social order where political power openly trumps sovereignty and law without blowback. You cannot then critique and understand the dynamics of this social order via discourses and worldviews that are not organic to this reality. Nor can you expect this social order to replicate a supposedly longed for and sought reality alien to it as the apparatuses and mechanism of power in existence render this reality an alien invader of the body politic.

The abiding reality of the testimonies of the public servants analysed is the fact that the ruling politicians of the day in their hegemony define what is illicit/licit by their actions and the impunity exercised and derived thereof. The ruling politicians of the day have then their own body of irregularities defined and exercised by themselves that they have made normal in the daily operations of government. For others in the social order to attempt similar actions without the express permission of the ruling politicians then they face the full power of the politicians applied to them. For the base rule is never challenge the hegemonic power of the ruling politicians. With reference to the rule of law an empty concept in itself the operative condition is impunity and in the realm of power relations it's the product of hegemonic power. The abiding lesson of the testimonies of the public servants is the extent to which they go to police themselves in the face of the hegemonic power of the ruling politicians and their irregularities/crimes. The rule of law and rightful duty are all subservient discourses used to mask the domination of and discipline of public servants by and to the hegemonic power of ruling politicians. What is also evident from the testimonies of public servants to the Senate Committee is the strictly policed hierarchy of the public service where those wielding power devote all their resources to ensure domination and discipline of those deemed threats even deviant/delinquents to their power. Specific public servants who by their actions constituted threats and were deemed deviant/delinquent testified as to the retribution expected or received and the need for their silence. The majority simply policed themselves and abided by the norms of the power relations. It's then obvious that the hegemonic power of the ruling politicians has constituted the internal power relations of the public servants in the quest for hegemony. In this quest on a daily power relations basis those connected to the politicians will exert power within the public service that has no connection to their official post in the structure of the public service with impunity being the benefit derived thereof. Power in the public service has been broken into a cellular structure which does not necessarily abide by the official static hierarchy of the public service by hegemonic political power. One can then be a Director of a department and have your juniors wielding power over you given their connection to a ruling politician.

The illicit enterprise of the ruling politicians in alliance with transnational organised crime has in the IND an operational mechanism of normalisation where norms to ensure the operational sustainability of the illicit enterprise define and police behaviour. In the context of power relations in this milieu a discourse of delinquency defines all those who refuse to abide by the hegemony of the illicit enterprise with those so defined disciplined and punished.

Summed up potently in the testimonies of Tench, Castellanos, Pacheco and Valdez.

The Ruling Politicians before the Senate Committee

To be complete this study must then analyse the testimonies of ruling politicians who appeared before the Senate Committee with the express task of deconstructing the discourses utilised.

In May 2017 Elvin Penner former Minister of State in the Ministry of Immigration was the first ruling politician to appear before the Senate Committee. Penner read from a prepared statement stating as follows: "Having duly being acquitted by a competent court of Belize, the Wong Hong Kim episode is to be regarded as a closed chapter, as a lawyer would say, 'Res Judicata.' And I will not be responding to any questions relating to that issue and or to any related issue which could have been the subject of the criminal prosecution that concluded." Penner continues as follows: "Having laid out the rights and privileges afforded to me under the law, I am now prepared to furnish a response to any questions that are legally permissible and questions that are relevant to the Auditor General's Special Report." Penner is response to questions from the Committee denied the accuracy of the testimony of Gordon Wade to the Committee and admitted that he knew personally Wong Hong Kim having met and interacted with him in Taiwan and China but never in Belize. The Committee then moved on to the case of the Turkish national Yakup Sut who received his Belizean nationality certificate and a Belizean passport via the same process as Wong Hong Kim. Penner admitted to the Committee that he did sign the nationality certificate for Sut but had no evidence that Sut was a resident of Belize. Penner stated in his testimony that he first met Sut in Los Angeles, California, USA and in Germany. In response to the allegations of the audit report that he back dated his signature on the Sut nationality certificate Penner stated the IND failed to use the files in numerical sequence. On the question of Penner signing a nationality certificate for an applicant who was exempted from the process of investigation and examination to ensure they qualified for nationality Penner stated that he assumed Sut was in Belize and it's the duty of the IND to ensure that applicants do qualify. Other than these replies Penner stuck to his opening position. On Penner's second appearance at the Committee he again read from a prepared statement with the same position on the questions posed by the Committee as with his first appearance. After two appearances Penner revealed nothing of substance to the Committee adopting the discourse of sovereignty and law to indicate that he was in fact sovereign and under no obligation of duty to the state of Belize. Penner utilised this discourse to justify silence on his actions at a time when he was a Minister of State in the government of Belize, a member of the House of Representatives and a member of the ruling UDP. The message is then potently clear as to the power wielded by ruling politicians over the state of Belize.

http://amandala.com.bz/news/elvin-penner-shuts-won-hong-kim/

http://amandala.com.bz/news/penner-approved-nationality-certificate/

http://www.reporter.bz/front-page/penner-dont-ask-me-about-kim/

http://amandala.com.bz/news/penner-cabinet-list-exist-pm-barrow-doesnt-remember/

http://www.reporter.bz/business/penner-back-at-senate-hecklers-make-mischief/

Carlos Perdomo the Cabinet Secretary and former Minister of National Security was the second ruling politician to appear before the Committee. Perdomo was questioned on the testimony of Therese Chavarria to the Committee of the issue of the issuing of a passport to Paul Ku. Perdomo denies all knowledge of the Paul Ku case as follows: "I did not give any directive, as the report says, to the director of immigration, and I would like to say that when I was briefed about this situation, the whole scenario was already completed, because nobody, at least from what was briefed to me orally, I did not know anything about this case." Perdomo denies knowledge of the Paul Ku case therefore he was not involved. Perdomo continues: "my first thing is to read the minute, and if the minute would ever say not all the papers are there and so, I would not sign it. So even though some of them have proven to be fraudulent, I would always look for two minutes, one from the officer in charge of the section, and one from the Director. And once they tell me all is in order, they meet legal requirements, and I would sign it." Perdomo did encounter applications with fraudulent documents or missing documents which he refused to sign. Then there are those he signed on the directions of senior employees of the IND as he took their word as being trustworthy. Any problems with these applications are not his fault. Perdomo states: "I wasn't aware that there was a culture of corruption, but in every talk with friends and so, you hear about customs, you hear about immigration, you hear about police, so that is how you hear. But I wasn't aware that there was a culture within the department, but you would hear jokes like this one got big house, like so...I did not know there was the operative type of thing." The agencies of the state are corrupt but a ruling politician, Perdomo, doesn't know about it and his knowledge of it is based on hearsay from his friends and jokes he is privy to as Perdomo is ignorant of the reality. Perdomo is then stating that he is the hostage of corrupt agencies of the state, powerless to break the dominance of these agencies over the ruling politicians. Hence the adoption of the methodology he outlined for treating with IND documents that required his approval. Perdomo is then the victim not the dominant politician commanding staff of the IND to facilitate his irregularities. Perdomo in his testimony to the Committee made clear his position on the testimony of Therese Chavarria to the Committee. Perdomo states: "Apparently, according to reports, she knew a lot of things, she was supposedly bribed, but nobody knew of that. She went on vacation, took files at home, which is pretty irregular, but nobody knew anything of that until she came back, and it is after everything is complete, passport signed, blah, blah, blah, that she makes a report after vacation." Perdomo launches an attack on the integrity of Chavarria with the clear intent of discrediting her testimony but more importantly to send a message to public servants who dared to violate the norms of the power relation where they are dominated and expected to be docile.

Perdomo in his testimony unleashes a discourse of three discursive lines: that of rightful duty, that of being victim to public servants as they are dominant and the contrary discursive line of policing the power relation to root out challenges to the domination of ruling politicians. The message of domination and expected docility to public servants is masked by the discursive lines of rightful duty and the ruling politician as victim. Blood masked by smiles simply an evolved version of the colonial discourse of "Smiles and Blood".

http://amandala.com.bz/news/cabsec-carlos-perdomo-badmouths-therese-chavarria/

http://www.reporter.bz/front-page/ex-minister-perdomo-to-senate-i-did-nothing-wrong/

http://www.reporter.bz/front-page/chan-takes-the-stand-perdomo-reappears-before-senate/

In July 2017 Ministers Edmond Castro and Anthony Martinez testified before the Committee. Castro and Martinez refused to answer the following questions: those arising from the testimony before the Committee of Alvarine Burgess, any questions which didn't deal with the content of the audit report. They also attacked the credibility of Burgess as a witness where Castro dismissed her testimony as hearsay, lies and political persecution at the hands of the opposition PUP. Castro proceeded to ask questions of Senators posing questions to them on their illicit actions as stealing electricity and/or water, sexual assault and their political agenda to persecute him. Castro responded to questions arising from the testimony of Burgess by Senator Chebat as follows: "That's PUP smoke. You guys are so desperate to get into power you are trying to create fire when there is no fire."

Some would say that both Ministers were on the attack in an attempt to scuttle the questioning of the Committee but what is apparent from the dialogue is the arrogance exhibited born out of the impunity enjoyed by the ruling politicians of the day in Belize. Theirs was a nuanced repeat of the Elvin Penner strategy focused on shock and awe via aggression. The strategy employed had the desired effect as nothing of substance was revealed by both Ministers.

http://www.reporter.bz/front-page/sparks-fly-as-castro-and-boots-testify/

http://amandala.com.bz/news/castro-attempts-castrate-senate-inquiry/

http://amandala.com.bz/news/we-expect-ministers-disrespectful-senator-elena-smith/

On May 30, 2017 in a press release Edmond Castro stated that he was informed by the US Embassy to Belize that his diplomatic and tourist visas were revoked and that Castro was invited to visit the embassy to re-apply for a US visa which he declined as he had no interest in travelling to the US. This press release preceded Castro's appearance at the Senate Committee in July 2017. The US Embassy gave no reason in public for the cancellation of Castro's US visas. Prime Minister Dean Barrow in public is reported in reporter.bz as having said that the US Embassy didn't brief him on the revocation of Castro's visas and he found it strange that no reason was given for the revocation. In addition, the Prime Minister does not believe that the US Embassy has a recording of Castro involved in the process of selling visas for a fee for if they did the Embassy would have informed the Prime Minister of this recording and they never did. For the Prime Minister the revocation of Castro's visas has nothing to do with impropriety on Castro's part.

A strategy of damage control driven by a discourse aimed at propagating a view of the operational choices and methodologies of the US state agencies which doesn't match with the operational reality and choices of these US Federal agencies. A discourse then of deception for the purpose of maintaining political dominance in the electoral politics of Belize. Betraying the perception that political damage was being done to the government and the UDP by the public revelations of the illicit enterprise of the IND.

http://www.reporter.bz/front-page/us-strips-castro-of-diplomatic-and-tourist-visas/

http://amandala.com.bz/news/hon-edmond-castro-explains-cancellation-visas/

Cabinet Ministers Rene Montero and Manuel Heredia Jr appeared before the Senate Committee in July 2017. Montero when questioned on a letter dated January 9, 2012 to the then Director of Immigration Montero said: "At no time did I infer that they shouldn't follow the vetting process or that they should proceed with incomplete applications, at no time did I infer that or alluded to that, it was simply a request to facilitate," Montero then pleads his innocence to charges of running an immigration hustle. Heredia Jr was questioned on the volume of recommendations he made for members of the Harmouch family to be granted visas. Heredia Jr insisted that he made recommendations for applicants from the Harmouch family and inquiries into the status of these applications but never requested to view these files personally. Heredia Jr then also denied that he was part of the immigration hustle. Heredia Jr states as follows: "I would never request a file. What I usually do and have been doing for, like I said, from the time I have been mayor of the island until now, if they give me a copy of their receipt, I will go and find out if what, if anything is missing...and I will advise the person accordingly." This is then the extent of Heredia Jr's public service not organised crime. Heredia Jr then reveals his second discursive line as follows: "My job is to recommend. If there are irregularities in the application, that is not my job to check, it is the job of the officers in charge to check. Something was wrong, then they should have not qualified this person, I have never instructed, or will not ever instruct anyone, to say, 'look he does not qualify, we'll go ahead and grant.' I will never do with that." Heredia Jr utilised his discourse without wavering in the face of the questioning by the members of the Committee. Heredia Jr's discourse of rightful duty defined as public service as an elected politician and the failings of public servants amounts to don't blame him for the failure of public servants at the IND to do their jobs effectively. The public servants at the IND were negligent of their rightful duty unlike him.

http://www.reporter.bz/front-page/two-more-ministers-before-senate-committee/

http://amandala.com.bz/news/im-innocent-blame-immigration-department-irregularities-hon-manuel-heredia-jr/

The final Minister of Government to appear before the Senate Committee was Godwin Hulse Minister of Immigration since 2012. Hulse read a statement to the Committee following which he was questioned by the Committee. In his statement Hulse apologised to Belize for any embarrassment caused by the revelations of the illicit acts of the visa and passport hustle in recent years. Hulse indicated that in response to the illicit acts the IND had set in train processes to stamp out corruption within the IND. Hulse states: "We took a vigorous process to try to set in place some systems to correct these wrongs and to prevent recurrence as far as is humanly possible." On the issue of applicants recommended by Ministers of Government Hulse stated that such recommendations are not necessary to the processes at IND and no public servant at IND must be fearful of refusing to honour said recommendations. On the power structure of the IND concerning applications Hulse states: "The person applies, especially in the case of the Chinese. They pay their $2,000, there are some requirements that need to be met and the director can say no-and the director can say no-and I did hear on the stand where persons were talking about intimidation-does not apply to the director. The director is appointed properly, the director cannot be removed, and if she is transferred she or he has to be given another head of department position within the structure here or sent home and paid off until retirement. So I really don't buy that at all." On the nature of demand for illicit IND services Hulse states: "There are only two reasons, to my mind, that someone pays and is involved in any corrupt activity: one is to expedite a process, and one is to circumvent a process." "So I could not see paying to expedite that process in nationalities. So clearly, it has to be the latter, which is to pay to get a process done for which you did not qualify."

Hulse appears at the Committee hearing seeking to mend fences and reassure the public that the breach has been sealed at the IND. He admits that there were in fact illicit acts at the IND and insists that the government has responded responsibly to ensure that these acts no longer occur. This is the discourse of rightful duty by the government and Hulse as Minister with responsibility for the IND. He then assures the public servants of the IND that they can disregard Ministerial recommendations for applicants by stressing on the power and responsibility of the Director. The Director is then charged with the task of ensuring the integrity of the process which is then the rightful duty of the post not the ruling politician. Illicit acts within the IND will result in the Director being held responsible. But Hulse states that a Director can be transferred whilst retaining the status of a director to another department or sent home but not removed. But what is the difference in daily work reality? Herein lies the message from Hulse to public servants. The defining statement of Hulse is his recognition that the basis of the illicit acts at the IND is framed by organised crime for to purchase illicit services which you don't qualify for from a state agency is in fact organised crime. In the face of the demand from organised and transnational organised crime Hulse has then thrown the public servants of the IND under the bus especially the post of Director who is now the fall guy of the department. The discourse of Hulse was devised to deliver political messages to various audiences: the supporters of the government, international powers, the public servants, the opposing political forces and most important to transnational organised crime. The discursive line of rightful duty arising from sovereignty and law drove the discourse but did this discourse indicate that the immigration and passport hustle was now dead? Or did it indicate that there must be now an ordered access to services as the helter skelter feeding frenzy now constitutes a grave threat to the sustainability of the organised crime enterprise?

http://www.reporter.bz/front-page/godwin-hulse-apologizes-for-immigration-hustle/

The most noteworthy statement made by a ruling politician of Belize on the audit report of the IND was not made via testimony to the Senate Special Committee but by Prime Minster (PM) Dean Barrow in public and reported by the media in 2016. According to the media report PM Barrow stated that a joint-select committee of the National Assembly/House of Representatives will be appointed instead of a Senate committee. On speaking of the audit report of the office of the Auditor General the PM stated that his government accepts the majority of the findings of the report but the report had major discrepancies. Barrow states: "It never gave the Department the opportunity to respond to and clear up allegations which had legitimate explanations. And it sure as hell did not follow the rules of natural justice in naming people as wrong doing without ever giving them a chance to answer or even comment on the accusation." Barrow stated that this breach of natural justice by the office of the Auditor General would make it very difficult for criminal convictions to be realised against persons identified in the audit report. Barrow sends the message that any failure to convict on criminal charges persons named in the audit report is the responsibility of the Auditor General not the product of the lack of will of the government. Even before the investigation of the joint-select committee of the House of Assembly commences the PM has potently defined the political terrain in which action on the content of the audit report will be executed. That Barrow will at the end of 2016 change his position on his choice of a joint-select committee of the House of Representatives to that of a Special Committee of the Senate to investigate the content of the audit report is indicative of the reaction to his decision especially by the Belize National Teachers Union (BNTU) and their 11-day strike in October 2016 for better governance and Belizean civil society. The audit report placed online and the report available in Belize are in fact widely different as the names of those accused of wrong doing are excised from the online version of the report.

http://www.reporter.bz/front-page/barrow-promises-investigation-into-findings-of-immigration-audit/

http://amandala.com.bz/news/bntu-ready-rumble/

Senate Committee hearings

The abiding lesson of the testimonies before the Senate Committee of the public servants and the ruling politicians who testified is the finger pointing and allocation of blame for the morass at the IND between both groups. The public servants utilised the discourse of being victims of the ruling politicians and their organised crime enterprise and in rebuttal the ruling politicians utilised the discourse of being victims at the hands of powerful, incompetent and politically motivated public servants. Both discourses utilised address the political terrain of Belize as they are constructed as political discourses to assault and defend in a bid to disarm entities locked in a power relation. But the entities locked in the power struggle are not comparable entities in the exercise of power in the social order. What then is the minimum attainable outcome for the public servants serving up this discourse? Is it a new operational methodology that ensures the sustainability of the illicit enterprise at the IND?

In spite of the battle of the discourses both groups in their testimonies didn't present prosecutable evidence in support of their discursive positions and it's still to be determined if they will do so. The outcome of this discursive game before the Senate Committee is the continued sustainability of the working organised crime alliance at the IND between the TCOs of Belize, the ruling politicians and public servants. The sustainability of this illicit enterprise is the paramount concern of those in the alliance.

Cases of Interest external of the Audit Report

The case of the use of Coast Guard vessels

Specific cases external of the power relations enmeshing the audit report of the IND including the investigation by the Special Senate Committee reveal the expanse of the spaces of the power relations of transnational organised crime, ruling politicians and the state agencies of Belize within the social order of Belize. And the actions of ruling politicians which illustrate their worldview, operational environment and the level of impunity enjoyed. In a news report dated June 1, 2017 PM Barrow stated that the Minister of Defence John Saldivar can no longer use the Coast Guard vessels that were a gift of the USA to Belize to transport the basketball team Saldivar owns, the Bandits, fans and relatives to and from games in San Pedro. PM Barrow stated that he was impressed that the Commander of the Coast Guard, Rear Admiral John Borland was in agreement with Saldivar that there was nothing wrong in using the said vessels to transport Saldivar's team and its retinue. But Barrow said he would not have done it and "that cannot be done again...That sort of use is now completely and absolutely off the table." This public statement of PM Barrow follows the public position of the US Embassy to Belize on the use of Coast Guard vessels by the Bandits organisation owned by John Saldivar, Minister of Defence. The US Embassy in the news report stated that it was aware of the reports of the inappropriate use of the said vessels by the Bandits organisation and that it was gathering further information on the use of the vessels. The US Embassy stated: "The US government has provided training and equipment, including boats to the Belize Coast Guard. The primary purpose of these vessels is to deter and interdict criminal activity, particularly in response to counter-narcotics efforts." The press report states that the Bandits organisation comprises a basketball, a football and a softball team all scheduled to play in San Pedro and that on occasions up to three Coast Guard vessels with their personnel and consuming fuel donated by the US have been used in the service of the Bandits organisation. In response to the news report which carried the position of the US Embassy on the use of the vessels the Ministry of Defence and Minister of Defence John Saldivar issued a press release on the issue of the use of the vessels. The press release states: "The Ministry makes clear that the deployment of armed forces assets are the responsibility of the Commanders of the armed forces who are completely aware of the purpose to which they are to be used. In cases where these assets are donated for the primary use of deterring crime and detecting illegal activities which are in line with the Defence Mandate, the Commanders of the BCG and the Belize Defence Force (BDF) may deploy them for other activities as they see fit." The press release then stated that the Ministry is a supporter of sporting activities seen in the sporting teams fielded by the BCG and the BDF hence its support for the Bandits sporting organisation. John Saldivar in a post to his Facebook page stated: "There is absolutely no misuse in using public resources to help a basketball team and I am absolutely prepared to go down believing that!!! If it is acceptable to use BTL and BTB funds to sponsor a Machel Montano concert, how can it be a misuse of public resources to assist a basketball team with transportation to San Pedro?" The political discourse of PM Barrow and Minister Saldivar strikingly flows with the discourse utilised by the ruling politicians who testified before the Senate Committee. The discourse of the power of the public servants and the ruling politicians being powerless in the face of this power is utilised as at the hearings of the Senate Committee. The Commander of the Coast Guard has the power over the vessels and their allocation therefore the Minister cannot compel the Commander to supply up to three vessels with donated fuel in the service of the Bandits organisation. The Commander did so out of his support for sport. That the Bandits organisation is owned by the Minister is simply of no consequence, irrelevant. There are no limits to the power of the ruling politician and when this impunity creates political problems you simply deploy the political spin machine. PM Barrow deploys the same discourse when he states that the Commander approved of the use of the vessels, he applauds him for seeing the need to support the sporting team but with immediate effect it must not happen again without reason given. The PM has then placed a limit to the power of the Minister not law it's a personal exercise of power arising from a power relation rooted in politics. But unanswered questions persist such as: what other non-Coast Guard personnel were given access to the US donated vessels? Were the gaps in the coastal border defence of Belize created with the diversion of up to three vessels to service the Bandits organisation fully exploited by transnational organised crime in Belize?

http://www.reporter.bz/front-page/pm-to-saldivar-stop-using-coast-guard-boats/

http://www.reporter.bz/general/saldivardefense-ministry-respond-to-allegations-of-misuse-of-public-assets/

http://www.reporter.bz/front-page/us-embassy-taking-note-of-ministers-misappropriation-of-donations/

The case of the BDF uniforms

In July 2017 a news report stated that a Belizean national was found with close to 100 uniforms of the BDF as a result of a raid on his Orange Walk residence close to the Belize-Mexico border. A Mexican national on his way to the Mexican border with Belize was interdicted with a number of BDF uniforms in his possession and arrested. The Mexican national subsequently revealed to authorities that the source of the uniforms was the Belizean national in Orange Walk whose home was raided by authorities. Both individuals were released without being charged. CoP Whylie stated that persons were no longer charged in Belize for being in possession of BDF uniforms illegally as it was not a crime. There is then in Belize no illegal possession of a BDF uniform. The news report stated that 1200 BDF uniforms were written off as they were unserviceable and the Belizean national of Orange Walk was one such person contracted to dispose of the said uniforms. The Belizean national therefore kept in his possession uniforms marked for disposal and was offering them for sale which is not a crime in Belize. The reality of this act of disposal is that in the border zone of the Belize-Mexico border where the gangland affiliates of the MTTOs exercise hegemony over this trafficking transition zone genuine BDF uniforms are available and for sale. Thereby facilitating the operational depth of gangland in this transition zone towards further shrinking the presence of the Belizean state and enhancing the hegemony of the MTTOs in this transition zone. Operational incompetence, operational denial or a joint enterprise with transnational organised crime?

http://amandala.com.bz/news/cartels-fake-military-uniforms/

The case of Yuanran Zheng

Yuanran Zheng entered Belize from the US in November 2017. Accompanied by his translator, a Taiwanese resident of Belize, Zheng presented a nationality certificate of Belize at the Social Security Board's (SSB) headquarters in Belmopan in his application for his social security card necessary to apply for a Belizean passport. The IND declared Zheng's nationality certificate to be a forgery as it was not of the type issued since May 2017 and there is no record at the IND of Zheng being issued a nationality certificate. Zheng was arrested, charged and fined in the Magistrates' courts where he promptly paid his fines and voluntarily left Belize for Canada where he resides. In a raid on the living quarters of his translator fraudulent SSB cards were seized. Given the operational history of the IND as exposed by the audit report what is defined as a fraudulent nationality certificate? Was Zheng's nationality certificate issued after May 2017 or before the IND cannot say as no record of the Zheng transaction was found. Was Zheng's nationality certificate issued by the IND before May 2017 and no record exists at the IND as Zheng was as Wong Hong Kim and David Nanes illicit recipients of nationality certificates for which they didn't qualify but paid the price? In the aftermath of the audit report and the hearings of the Senate Committee the damage control methodology now calls for selective seizure and prosecution for "fraudulent" IND documents. The seizure of "fraudulent" SSB cards led to an investigation which uncovered three more "fraudulent" nationality certificates at the SSB which pointed to the circulation of nationality certificates and other documents that were used under the defunct Economic Citizenship Program of the 1990s. Again instances of the operations of the joint enterprise with transnational organised crime in spite of the audit report and the political posturing in which the IND and the SSB are implicated.

http://www.reporter.bz/front-page/chinese-men-busted-with-fake-nationality-documents/

http://amandala.com.bz/news/chinese-national-yuanran-zheng-accomplice-nabbed-immigration-fraud/

http://amandala.com.bz/news/chinese-yuanran-zheng-45-paid-1800-fine-fraudulent-nationality-certificate-left-belize/

The case of William Donny Mason

The discovery of the head on ice in a bucket of Llewellyn Lucas of Dandridge, Belize in a pickup truck owned by William Mason in July 2016 set in train a course of events that would impact the government of PM Barrow. William Mason otherwise known as Raj Ouelett, Danny Ouelett, Ramesh Ouelett and William Ferguson is originally a Guyanese citizen deported from Canada as a result of criminal activity who then appeared in Belize. In Belize Ouelett/Mason acquired a Belizean birth certificate attesting that he was born in Belize and subsequently was granted several gun licenses which gave him the legal permission to own firearms. Ouelett/Mason was reputedly connected to several ruling politicians of the UDP government but specific evidence in the public domain links Mason to three Ministers. He is an investor in the Bandits Football Club of Minister of Defence, John Saldivar, financier of the successful 2015 by-election campaign of Minister of State, Frank Mena and has access to Deputy PM and Minister of Education Patrick Faber. He is also a financier of the ruling UDP political party. The charges of murder and of kidnapping placed on Ouelett /Mason and his accomplices emanate from being involved in among other things extortion enterprises targeting males from the Mennonite congregation of Belize. Where according to public statements of the police two Mennonite males, David Dodd and Lloyd Thiessen, met with Ouelett/Mason to finalise business deals during the course of which they were kidnapped and extorted. In the course of the meeting with Dodd, Llewelyn Lucas was kidnapped, murdered and his corpse supposedly burnt. The extortion of Thiessen and his wife preceded the Dodd sting by some two months but Thiessen and his wife fled from Belize after their release. Why the choice of Lucas to take and keep with the intent to display his head? This is a practice of gangland affiliates of the MTTOs. Why wasn't Thiessen's and Dodd's heads taken? Who then gave up Ouelett/Mason calling for his demise?

In August 2016 Amandala.com.bz published an article on an interview the newspaper held with Ouelett/Mason via telephone from the remand yard. In the article Ouelett/Mason states: "These guys are trying to frame me and I have a lot of information about them." Ouelett/Mason is stating by his discourse that he is innocent and is sending a warning to those in power who are associates of his that he will not go down in silence. Ouelett/Mason in the interview names his immediate target for the interview who are the Police officer commanding the Eastern Division Rural, ACP Edward Broaster and the Police officer commanding the Hattieville Police Station, Assistant Superintendent Rochelle Chan, which is in the Eastern Division Rural. Ouelett/Mason in the interview insisted that the Eastern Division Rural commander through the officer in charge of the Hattieville police station made repeated requests for donations from him. Ouelett/Mason states: "I've never met Mr Broaster, and Mr Broaster is the one that actually sends messages to the Hattieville Police Station's Inspector Chan to get me to donate motorcycles and homes to them. I've donated a lot of stuff." Inspector Chan told Amandala that he met with Ouelett/Mason during a police investigation and Ouellet/Mason offered to help the police. Chan then requested motor vehicles and a new structure to house the Mahogany Heights police station but Ouelett/Mason failed to deliver. It's then the word of Ouelett/Mason against the publicly stated position of Commander of the Eastern Division Rural (Broaster) and the Officer in charge of the Hattieville police station (Chan). Ouelett/Mason in the interview makes a statement that illustrates his messages to various audiences in Belize as follows: "The people of Belize need to know, they need answers and for the citizens of Belize I am prepared to make sure they know the answers. This corruption, crimes against humanity, all these other things need to stop. There are people who are starving in this country who are living below the poverty line. I am the only guy, I know right now is hiring people, paying people, helping people, always delivering what I need to deliver and not one of these police can ever say that I ever said no to them, including the Ministers. Everyone will say that my character speaks for itself." Ouelett/Mason has indicated that he is now willing and able to be an informer, a whistle blower for the people of Belize to be informed of his relationship with the police and the ministers of government. Ouelett/Mason is the Patron of Belize as he does right by all who seek his intervention never having failed to deliver. This then is the potency of his threat to expose in public his relationship with the powerful for he has delivered without fail to the police and ministers and they have now failed him as he is incarcerated. This grave act of ingratitude and treachery has now forced his hand to now break the cardinal rule against being an informer.

In the Amandala news report ACP Edward Broaster stated that in 2014 whilst investigating a complaint against Ouelett/Mason he became aware of Ouelett's/Mason's criminal career in Canada and he informed the Commissioner of Police of it but not John Saldivar then Minister of National Security with responsibility for the Police. The question arises as to when did Ouelett/Mason receive approval from the Commissioner of Police for his gun licences and if after being informed of Ouelett's/Mason's criminal record in Canada what was done with reference to his eligibility to be a holder of gun licences?

Ouelett/Mason is a product of the social order that thrives as a result of the operational space granted to the joint enterprise between transnational organised crime, ruling politicians and agents of the state. Where an individual with the requisite access can build an illicit operational network in the social order as it is facilitated by the very nature of the social order and the state form. And with time this individual will develop linkages with the licit sector and its agencies which embolden the actions of the individual to the point where he begins to feed off individuals and groups in the joint enterprise and outside of it. When licit action is demanded as there is a choice available and set in train the arrested individual can levy damage on the licit order by dint of the linkages developed with the licit order. The individual is simply publicly mouthing threats to secure a settlement that serves the interests of both sides: the ruling politicians and the individual. The entire scenario is highly reminiscent of the case of Shahid Roger Khan in Guyana.

The revelations in public of the links of Ouelett/Mason to ruling politicians added to the impetus of the BNTU on the issue of good governance to engage with the government via a national strike of Belizean teachers which went into effect from the 3rd to 14th October 2016. In August and October of 2016 the PM again reshuffled his Cabinet for a grand total of four times in 2016 following a general elections victory in 2015 with an increased majority over that of the 2012 general elections. In the August reshuffle the armed forces were moved to the new Ministry of Defence under Minister John Saldivar whilst the Police was placed in the Ministry of Home Affairs which during 2016 saw a shuffling of Ministers. In 2016 Minister Faber became Deputy Prime Minister, John Saldivar retained his seat in the Cabinet and Edmund Castro returned to the Cabinet. What became apparent in 2016 is the limited number of face cards in the pack of politicians of the UDP that PM Barrow is willing to play. The number of face cards was also diminished by resignations from ministerial posts and politics in general by members of the Cabinet. At the time of writing the Ouelett/Mason trial is yet to commence.

http://www.reporter.bz/front-page/highlights-of-2016/

http://amandala.com.bz/news/william-mason-hot-hot-water/

http://amandala.com.bz/news/william-mason-speaks-amandala-prison/

http://amandala.com.bz/news/10-top-2016-stories/

The Case of Gaspar Vega former Minister and Deputy Prime Minister

A news report dated 19 October 2016 on Amandala.com presented the details of a land deal involving Andre Vega, son of then Minister of Lands, Gaspar Vega and the Lands Department of the Ministry of Lands as presented by the then Attorney General Vanessa Retreage. The details of the land transaction presented by the then Attorney General details an organised crime enterprise in the Ministry of Lands. The details are as follows: On June 8, 1988 Carlton Russell legally sold 2.2 acres of land situated near to the mouth of the Belize River to Miguel Valencia for BZ$ 50,000. The 2.2 acres of land were privately owned not state lands therefore the Department of Lands had no legal right to dispose of said land. On August 25, 2011 Sharon Pitts applied to lease 2.75 acres of land along the Northern Highway in Belize City. On August 31, 2011 Pitts received permission to survey 1.5 acres of the said land. In October 2011 the Lands Commissioner was informed that the said portion of land was already owned privately therefore not by the state as it was surveyed and recorded in the survey register. The Lands Commissioner then instructed the National Estate Officer to revoke the permission granted to Pitts to survey the said parcel of land. Pitts was so informed by letter dated November 3, 2011.

In spite of the letter of November 3, 2011 Pitts proceeded to survey the said land and submitted the survey plan to the Lands Department which examined, authenticated it, approved it and duly recorded it in the survey register. A note from the Lands department was placed in the Pitts file which stated that the Pitts survey of October 20, 2011 superseded the previous survey plan in the register. There was no record at the Lands Department as to the identity of the public servant who approved the Pitts survey plan. On November 11, 2016 Pitts was issued a lease for the land by the Lands Department. On November 25, 2011 the Lands Commissioner issued a letter stating the questions over the ownership of the land hence its availability for distribution Pitts was issued a lease for which was countered by public servants in the mapping department of the Lands Department who insisted that the parcel of land leased to Pitts was state land. On November 30, 2011 the Minister of Natural Resources Gaspar Vega approved the sale of the parcel of land to Pitts for BZ$ 10,569. On September 24, 2012 Pitts took possession of the parcel of land as the owner by purchase agreement with the state. In the Pitts file at the Lands department minutes 7 to 25 are missing according to the then Attorney General. On January 17, 2012 Hilmar Alamilla received permission to survey 1.124 acres of land along the Philip Godson Highway but there is no evidence on file that Alamilla did in fact apply for a lease at the Lands Department. On November 28, 2011 the survey plan for the parcel of land was done for Alamilla and on December 6, 2012 it was examined, authenticated and approved by the Lands Department. On December 12, 2012 Alamilla applied to lease the said parcel of land. On January 15, 2013 the Commissioner of Lands and Survey recommended the sale of the parcel of land to Alamilla for BD$ 6,171 to the Minister of Lands Gaspar Vega. The Minister advised via note attached to the land purchase approval for Alamilla that the sale price be amended downwards to BD$ 2,500 which was reflected in the new land purchase approval dated January 29, 2013. Alamilla paid the price of the land and became the owner on May 7, 2013 and on December 30, 2013 sold the parcel of land for BD$ 15,000 to Andre Vega son of Gaspar Vega.

On December 9, 2014 the legal counsel in the Lands Department advised that an investigation be carried out to confirm that the land owned by Vega and Pitts in fact belonged to Valencia thereby confirming it was not state lands and could not be distributed. On December 15, 2014 the then acting principal surveyor of the Lands department confirmed by memo that the Vega and Pitts parcels of land did in fact belong to Valencia. By January 26, 2015 the surveyors who prepared the survey plan for the Vega parcel and the Pitts were informed in writing that their once approved and authenticated survey plans were cancelled thereby reinstating the Valencia survey plan as the substantive survey plan for the parcels of land. For the loss of land that was not the Ministry of Natural Resources own to sell to Pitts the Government of Belize paid BD$ 400,000 to Pitts as compensation for losing the said parcel of land. On July 27, 2015 by way of letter the Commissioner of Lands informed Andre Vega that his ownership of the said parcel of land was now invalid and reports indicate that Vega was now willing to surrender the parcel of land which he did not own legally for BD$ 400,000 which the Government of Belize accepted and duly paid. The news report reported that the then Attorney General Vanessa Retreage stated that the files were processed in error, that the monies paid to Pitts and Andre Vega will be recovered by the government and the practise of compensation for irregularities in land transactions at the Ministry of Natural Resources (Lands) will cease until further notice. A case of organised crime utilising the operational procedures and structure of the Ministry of Natural Resources to exploit the resources of the Ministry of Natural Resources. In this organised crime enterprise specific public servants of the Ministry especially the Lands Department are complicit and part of a criminal conspiracy for self-enrichment. The questions arise of the expanse of the organised crime enterprise in the Ministry and if it matched or surpassed the scale of the organised crime enterprise at the IND. A news report in the Reporter.bz dated December 8, 2017 reported the audit of land compensation payments at the Ministry of Natural Resources under Minister Gaspar Vega by the Office of the Auditor General was then ongoing. Auditor General Dorothy Bradley indicated to the media that there was a lot of information outstanding that must be collected. The outcome of this audit is anticipated as the unavailability of evidence at the Ministry will stymie the production and release of an audit report worth its salt. The then Attorney General already alluded to missing minutes in the Pitts file which can be a harbinger of the reality on the ground.

http://amandala.com.bz/news/lands-departments-800000-scandal/

http://www.reporter.bz/front-page/land-department-audit-underway/

A news report in Amandala.com dated October 29, 2016 reported that the Dean Barrow UDP government from 2008 to 2016 made some BD$ 70.9 million in land acquisition/ land compensation charges to the budget of the Ministry of Natural Resources. For the period 2011 to 2016 BD$ 61.7 million was paid and from 2008 to 2010 BD$ 9.2 million was paid. Payments exploded then in 2011 with the trend continuing to 2016. The state of Belize legally acquires land from private owners that falls under land acquisition and former owners are compensated through the line item vote of the Ministry of Natural Resources. But land compensation also arose when the state sold land to private owners that was not state land and it was not legally acquired before the sale by the state and the legal rightful owner successfully re-claimed their property whether in court of not. The Ministry of Natural Resources then chose to compensate the loss of the person it sold illegally the land to with cash. In the news report it is reported that a significant proportion of the escalated payments for land compensation at the Ministry of Natural Resources was to compensate persons who were sold land by the Ministry illegally. This operational procedure facilitated one aspect of the organised crime enterprise. At the heart of the organised crime enterprise is allocating state lands to chosen recipients at special prices way below market value utilising men of straw as the first recipient from the state. The straw men then pass on the land to the beneficial owner at below market price rates. In the course of the evolution of the organised crime enterprise in the Ministry a feeding frenzy ensued where private land was now being stolen by the actions of public servants of the Ministry which set in train the push back from private owners. The Ministry then chose to exploit this push back by compensating those with public funds who were recipients of stolen land and lost said lands to their legal owners. The fact that Andre Vega son of the Minister of Natural Resources bought a parcel of land sold by the state to Hilmar Alamilla campaign manager and confidant of Gaspar Vega Minister of Natural Resources illustrates the impunity enjoyed by ruling politicians in Belize. The fact that Andre Vincent was paid BD$ 400,000 in compensation for the loss of the land that was not the property of the state to sell from the Ministry headed by his father was simply the cherry on top of the heavy dose of impunity.

http://amandala.com.bz/news/lands-departments-800000-scandal/

A news report inAmandala.com dated October 29, 2016 reported that a parcel of land supposedly over 2 acres in size covered in mangrove was sold on February 15, 2012 for BD$ 6,500 by the Ministry of Natural Resources to a developer at Placencia North was acquired by the government via the Ministry of Natural Resources on July 14, 2015 for BD$ 1 million. No reasons from the Ministry of Natural Resources were forthcoming on the need for acquisition of the parcel of mangrove and for the price paid to the developer especially in light of the price paid to the state for the parcel of land under mangrove and it remains under mangrove over three years later.

http://amandala.com.bz/news/1-million-land-sold-6540-30/

A news report in Amandala.com dated November 2, 2016 reported on the sale of state lands to Elvin Penner, his mother Lina Penner and his father Edward Penner in 2015 following Edward Penner's dismissal from the Cabinet in 2013 and his non-selection as a candidate of the UDP for the general election to the House of Representatives in 2015. The news report states that in June 2015 Lena Penner mother of Elvin Penner purchased from the government 36.70 acres of land in the Mountain Pine Ridge of Cayo district at the cost of BD$ 9,776 or BD$ 266 per acre for prime real estate of Belize. Edward Penner father of Elvin Penner purchased from the government in 2015 some 10.07 acres of prime land on Turnette island at a price of BD$ 26,000. On October 20, 2014 the price of the parcel of land was set at BD$ 69,000 but on October 26, 2015 the government reduced the price to BD$ 26,000 again a steal of a deal for prime land on Turnette Island. On June 12, 2012 Elvin Penner was approved to purchase 36.17 acres of land at Mountain Pine Ridge in Cayo district but the government did not finalise the sale price until June 1, 2015 at BD$ 9, 404.20 or BD$ 260 per acre. The single commonality to the three Penner land deals is their finalisation in 2015 the year of a general election where in the quest for an electoral victory there was the pressing need to have those thrown overboard to return to the UDP's drive for victory. In this case the politicisation of the land resources of Belize is then apparent.

http://amandala.com.bz/news/udp-land-shenanigans/

A news report in Amandala.com dated December 14, 2016 reported on the purchase of 1,600 acres of state lands by individuals on the Philip Godson Highway outside Carmelita in Orange Walk district. These individuals who purchased the state lands then sold their land to members of the family of Minister of Natural Resources Gaspar Vega. The government subdivided the 1,600 acres of farmland into 55 parcels and German Vega, the brother of then Minister Gaspar Vega and his company German Vega & Sons Import Ltd purchased 33 of the 55 parcels from its owners. The wife of Minister Gaspar Vega Mariline Vega purchased 14 parcels of land. What is noteworthy is that owners of plots that bordered each other agreed to sell to German Vega and the wife of Gaspar Vega thereby giving the Vega family contiguous holdings. The Ministry of Natural Resources sold parcels of land for as little as BD$800 to the highest at BD$ 8,939.38. One parcel of 91.95 acres was sold to Hilmar Alamilla for BD$ 3, 669.38 but on the transfer document the price of BD$ 8,937.38 was pencilled in at the top of the document. The parcel of land was transferred to Alamilla on June 21, 2011 and he sold it to Mariline Roxana Vega on November 23, 2011 for BD$ 23,000 according to the transfer document. According to the news report a number of the transfer documents for parcels of land did not contain the sale price but were approved and the sale price on the transfer document for the sale of state lands were crossed out and another sale price pencilled in at the top. The wife of Hilmar Alamilla Alma Alamilla received a parcel of 54.13 acres next to the parcel of her husband's and liker her husband she received her state land on June 21, 2011 at a price of BD$ 2, 777.67 which was marked out on the transfer document and BD$ 5, 271.67 pencilled in at the top. Alma Alamilla sold her parcel of land on November 23, 2011 for BD$ 23,000 to Mariline Vega as was the case with her husband. The news report reported that in at least nine instances said parcels of state lands were transferred to German Vega & Sons Limited before it was sold and transferred to the recipient of the state land. The recipient of said parcels of state lands became owner of said parcels on September 2, 2013 but the said parcels were sold to German Vega & Sons Limited on August 27, 2013. Under law these transfers were in fact illegal as German Vega & Sone Ltd was not the recipient of said state lands and did not pay the state for them but had ownership transferred by the Ministry of Natural Resources to this corporate entity. The actions of the Ministry under the leadership of Gaspar Vega insinuates the identity of the beneficial owner of the said nine plots of land as German Vega & Sons Ltd. What is obvious with these transactions is the existence of an organised crime enterprise in the Ministry of Natural Resources involving public servants which will serve whichever of the two dominant political parties of Belize is in power. This organised crime enterprise is the product of the politicisation of state lands in Belize where both dominant political parties utilise state lands as an instrument of patronage, political mobilisation and the creation and maintenance of solidarity with individuals, families and clans seen as vital to political sustainability. The Westminster model of government facilitates rather than hinders the development of the politicisation of state lands and the organised crime enterprise that has an operational presence in the relevant Ministry of government.

http://amandala.com.bz/news/cordel-drops-bombshell-house-lands-corruption/

The final instance to be considered of the organised crime enterprise in the Ministry of Natural Resources though not the last in the public domain involves the sale of three lots of privately owned land at Caye Caulker as state lands in 2009 for BD$ 2,500 each. All three lots of land were sold to Ignacio German Vega and Karen Vega, Eduardo Vega and Andre Vega in February 2010 for BD$ 30,000, BD$ 25,000 and BD$ 30,000 respectively. By way of compensation for the "error" made by the Ministry of Natural Resources for selling privately owned lots of land to individuals who then sold them to members of the family of Minister Gaspar Vega. The Vega family members were compensated as follows: Ignacio and Karen Vega 8.167 acres on Mosquito Caye, Corozal District in November 2014, Eduardo Vega 7.215 acres on Mosquito Caye, Corozal District in April 2015 with the compensation for Andre Vega if he received any yet to be determined. Mosquito Caye is in fact an island some 8.5 miles to the north west of San Pedro. The legality of the compensation to the Vegas is under question as Mosquito Caye was leased in 2007 to a party from Corozal by the then PUP government with this lease allegedly cancelled by Gaspar Vega on his appointment as Minister of Natural Resources in 2008 following the victory of the UDP at the polls. The news report in Amandala.com which reported on this land transaction quoted PM Dean Barrow on the questionable land transactions of his government as follows: "What it is, is what it is! You are able to document that people, on the face of it, legitimately got land and they ended up afterwards selling it to particular persons. I don't know that there is any actionable illegality there. But the implications and the conclusions that you have drawn are not anything I will argue with you over at all." The discourse of law and sovereignty for PM Barrow raises the question of "actionable illegality" with reference to the land deals involving members of the Vega family but the perception of land scams and political corruption inevitably arise and are much more politically relevant than the evasive use of the discourse of law. Hence the reason why there is no point of contention over the implications and conclusion drawn. Implications and conclusions as these heighten the imperative to manage voter expectations and mobilisation to ensure political sustainability. In October 2016 PM Dean Barrow announced publicly the resignation from the government of Gaspar Vega. In a news report on the Reporter.bz the PM is quoted as follows in speaking of Vega: "made clear that he recognises that in all the circumstances, especially given that his son became the 'owner' of one of the two parcels and was paid compensation after the facts were discovered in terms of the titles having issued in error…his position naturally became untenable." Vega fell on his sword for including his son in a land compensation hustle within the Ministry of Natural Resources. His grave mistake was to involve his offspring thereby allowing the political enemies of the government and the UDP the space to assault the political hegemony of the UDP, its political leader and PM. For that he would leave the government and his position as deputy political leader of the UDP would come under assault as his political career. PM Barrow continues speaking of Gaspar Vega: "I am extremely saddened by what has happened. Gaspar Vega was certainly with me as my deputy from when we first won in 2008 and before that he was one of the fiercest battlers and most effective leaders of the United Democratic Party. In addition to all that, he was and remains my personal friend. He is one of the most warm hearted, caring, genuine individuals that I had the good fortune to come across." Gaspar Vega for PM Barrow is an exceptional political ally and an individual but these words are spoken at his political funeral until the next general election where it will be revealed if Gaspar Vega is now politically interred. The departure of Gaspar

Vega from the Cabinet of Belize did not end the organic link between the Vega family and the UDP government seen in the awarding of a contract of BD$ 7, 995, 926.40 for the rehabilitation and improvement of the drainage infrastructure of just over 1 mile of Faber's Road to Imer Hernandez nephew of Gaspar Vega. This contract became necessary after a state owned company BIL failed miserably to execute the project of rehabilitating Faber's Road.

http://amandala.com.bz/news/is/

http://www.reporter.bz/front-page/vega-land-scandal-continues/

http://www.reporter.bz/front-page/lands-scandal-forces-vega-out/

http://www.reporter.bz/general/controversy-erupts-over-fabers-road-reconstruction-contract/

The actions of the Ministry of Natural Resources under the leadership of Minister Gaspar Vega is at the time of writing the subject of placing in the public domain of documents indicating that the family of Minister of Works Rene Montero was in receipt of land compensation to the tune of BD$ 3, 147, 683. A news report in Amandala.com and Reporter.bz in March 2018 indicated that John Briceno political leader of the PUP stated in public that the PUP had located the documents for eleven instances of land compensation in 2011 paid by the Ministry of Natural Resources to the family of Rene Montero. Yvette Montero the daughter of Rene Montero purchased seven acres of land for BD$ 3,080 located six miles north of Ambergris Caye. The Ministry of Natural Resources paid BD$ 245,000 in compensation to Yvette Montero for the loss of title to the said land. Yvette Montero purchased 10 acres of land in the Pervasion Enclave in Mountain Pine Ridge from the state for BD$ 2, 240 and was paid BD$ 80,000 in compensation. Miguel Montero a brother of Rene Montero was sold ten acres of land northwest of San Pedro for BD$ 4,400, four acres of land at northwest San Pedro for BD$ 1,760 and twenty acres at Pervasion Enclave in Mountain Pine Ridge for BD$ 4,428. For these three parcels of land Miguel Montero was paid BD$ 721,000 in compensation by the Ministry of Natural Resources. Ismael Montero a brother of Rene Montero was sold 10.2 acres of land at Pervasion Enclave, Mountain Pine Ridge for

BD$ 2,220 and was paid BD$ 82,352 in compensation for the said parcel of land. Jamie Montero a brother of Rene Montero purchased from the state five acres of land northwest of San Pedro for BD$ 2,200 and was paid BD$ 175,000 in compensation for the said land. Alejandro Montero a brother of Rene Montero purchased 10 acres of land in the Pervasion Enclave and was paid BD$ 80,000 in compensation but the grant number of the said parcel of land at the time of the report is yet to be located. Alejandro Montero also purchased four acres of land north of San Pedro for BD$ 1,760 and another five acres in the same area for BD$ 2,200 from the state. The sum of BD$ 395,000 was paid in compensation for the two said parcels of land. The recipients of compensation in the Montero family including the daughter of Minister Rene Montero were paid by government a total of BD$ 1,778, 352 plus seven percent interest of the sum from the date of acquisition or BD$ 1,369,331 for a total compensation of BD$ 3, 147, 683. These were payments approved by the Ministry of Finance under the PM and Minister of Finance Dean Barrow. These lands were acquired in 1998 before the 1998 general elections under the then UDP government. The PUP re-possessed the said lands sold to members of the Montero family following their victory at the 1998 general elections. Upon their return to power in 2008 the Dean Barrow led UDP government set about the task of compensating for the land sold to the Montero family members under a previous UDP government and re-possessed by a former PUP government with interest. A clear case of the politicisation of state lands which fosters the creation and operation of an organised crime enterprise in the Ministry of Natural Resources.

http://amandala.com.bz/news/sick-udp-land-compensation-hustle-uncovered/

http://www.reporter.bz/front-page/pup-exposes-3-14-million-udp-land-scandal/

An organised crime enterprise involving ruling politicians, public servants and their clients generates and dispenses impunity to participating and connected individuals within the social order influencing personal choices and behaviour that are criminal in nature but devoid of the order and discipline of transnational and local organised crime. The organised crime enterprise of the Ministry of Natural Resources under the UDP has produced examples of this reality in the public domain. In July 2017 Hilmar Alamilla was arraigned for the murder of Daniel Sosa at the Orange walk Magistrates' Court and placed in remand. This is the said Hilmar Alamilla who was the campaign manager of Gaspar Vega and named in two land sale deals where he sold state lands purchased from the Ministry of Natural Resources to members of the Vega family including Andre Vega the son of Gaspar Vega. Alamilla was also involved in the illicit rosewood reaping and sale of trade during the moratorium in Belize. An interdicted shipment of his was publicly burnt by the then Minister responsible for the rosewood stock of Belize. In September 2017 Gustavo Hernandez the witness to the murder of Daniel Sosa was gunned down gangland execution style using the ride by method on the San Antonio road, Orange Walk. This is in keeping with the underworld maxims: death to informers and no witness no conviction.

http://www.reporter.bz/crime/man-killed-in-ow-accusations-of-political-interference/

http://www.reporter.bz/crime/key-witness-in-high-profile-murder-trial-executed/

In 2013 the Ministry of Natural Resources led by Minister Gaspar Vega compulsorily acquired a portion of the private land owned by Michael Modiri at Frank's Eddy. The government acquired the said land without the knowledge and consent of Modiri. Eddy Paumen then built an almost mile long road on the said public property to transport tourists and patrons to his Dark Night cave operation on Paumen's property. In April 2016 the Supreme Court ruled that the action of the Ministry of Natural Resources with respect to Modiri's land was without valid basis with no credibility to the claim that the acquisition was for the public purpose. Paumen was trespassing on Modiri's land and compensation was ordered by the court to be paid by Paumen to Modiri. In 2015 the former Commissioner of Lands Wilbert Vallejos testified that Minister Gaspar Vega gave the instruction to seize the portion of Modiri's land for the public purpose that Paumen subsequently absorbed into his business operations. Before the delivery of the judgment on the land case Paumen was charged with conspiracy to murder Michael Modiri and with paying for an illicit firearm to be placed in a vehicle of Modiri and then calling in the crime to the police who stopped and searched the vehicle discovered the illicit firearm resulting in the passengers of the vehicle being charged and incarcerated including Modiri. Another case where the organised crime enterprise of the Ministry of Natural Resources has spawned the use of criminal terror and violence to suppress the rule of law in the social order.

http://www.reporter.bz/business/accused-mastermind-bradley-paumen-ordered-to-pay-300000-for-trespass/

http://www.reporter.bz/business/vega-denies-allegations-of-land-repossession-in-paumen-case/

http://www.reporter.bz/uncategorized/vega-says-he-did-not-give-directive-to/

The politicisation of state lands in Belize was necessary to utilise the granting of state lands at below market prices to individuals and families of political importance to ruling parties was seen as a necessary instrument of patronage, the payment for favours rendered, building political capital and most importantly a vital part of a discourse of voter mobilisation. Under the UDP in its unbroken rule from 2008 to 2018 at the time of writing the politicisation of land has now evolved into an organised crime enterprise with the illustrated ability to adopt and exhibit the violence common to organised crime enterprises. This organised crime enterprise located in the Ministry of Natural Resources is now impacting the rule of law in Belize in the furtherance of criminality from within a bastion of the rule of law according to the Constitution of Belize. It is then perfectly normal for Transnational Organised Crime (TOC) groups in Belize to exploit this organised crime enterprise acquiring the necessary tracts of land within the transition zones of Belize and in other areas designated as future transition zones in the name of straw men and ghosts. On these tracts of land, the operations of the MTTOs will create interlocking zones which in effect become no go areas for the state as they are alienated from the sovereign state and its rule of law manned by the gangland affiliates of the MTTOs. Ideal spaces for drug labs, smuggled humans, weapons, illicit fuel etc.

Transnational Crime, Ruling Politicians and Public Servants: The Power Relations

The operational space afforded transnational crime organisations (TCOs) in Belize by the politicians and agents of the state/public servants has afforded TCOs the opportunity to operate within the spaces of the state institutions and the political realm thereby deepening their presence in and their power wielded over the social order of Belize. This operational presence in the spaces of the state and political realm where the rule of law and sovereignty is implied to be hegemonic creates a terrain where the implied hegemonic power of the state and law is relentlessly challenged. TCOs create an alternate social order driven by alternate power relations with its own apparatus and instruments of normalisation. The heavily policed norms of the TCOs' social order are then in conflict with those of a state and a social order premised on the rule of law. In Belize it must be understood that there are a number of social spaces external of state institutional spaces where the TCOs exert power over and in some of those spaces they exert hegemonic power. The contested spaces of Belize namely the border zones with Mexico, Guatemala and the Caribbean Sea and specific areas within the urban expanse of Belize City are all under the control of the TCOs namely the Mexican Transnational Trafficking Organisations (MTTOs), their partners and gangland affiliates. In these spaces the state is a visitor, a partner of the MTTOs as it doesn't exert hegemony over these spaces. This reality is expressed via the power relations between the TCOs, the politicians and the public servants of Belize as indicated in the audit report of the IND. What is now apparent is that the operational presence in the contested spaces of Belize which includes its major port and airport of the TCOs is now linked to an operational presence within the state spaces and an operational presence within the oligarchs of Belize. For all intents and purposes the TCOs have now penetrated operationally the social order of Belize: the state institutions, the political space, the oligarchy at the apex of the social order and the diffused spaces of the workers, the poor and the underclass and by their strategies of normalisation they are erecting an alternate social order parallel to that of the licit social order.

The alternate illicit social order of the TCOs is then constituting individuals through its operational discourse and its attendant worldview who range from being rejecters of the licit order in pursuit of the Gangsta ideal to a range of individuals who utilise an entire gamut of strategies of bridging both worlds through various methods of compromise or shades of grey. The pressures to react to the presence exerted by the illicit order through the conceptualisation of a range of choices on offer for individual action testifies to the power exerted over the social order of Belize by the TCOs potently illustrated by the testimonies of those who appeared before the Senate Committee. What must be realised is the operational reality that the TCOs are not interested in replacing the licit order with an illicit order as they need a supplicant licit order to maximise the profits of the illicit order. A specific task is then placed on the shoulders of the ruling politicians and the agents of the state/public servants of Belize. Theirs is the task of ensuring that the licit order of Belize maintains the necessary level of vibrancy and relevance to the social order to maintain some semblance of the operational impact necessary to maintain the licit order needed by the illicit order. But there are power relations between both orders as actors on both sides dream of the personal benefits of hegemony summed up as the drive to warlordism which constitutes a rocky road. The balancing act of politicians in this constantly evolving force relation between two orders and the international power relations impacting Belize is by far the most problematic of the entire terrain of power in Belize. Ruling politicians must balance the drive to win elections again and again, their personal desires for power, wealth, pleasure etc. and the need to serve two diametrically opposed masters. This is a minefield that has gravely damaged TCOs in the past and some view with alarm getting into bed with politicians. But operational alliances are necessary between the illicit and licit orders and there is little choice in the matter. The issue for Belize in light of this is what strategies you utilise to minimise the grave risks posed to the TCOs especially the MTTOs by an alliance with ruling politicians?

From the audit report and the testimonies to the Senate Committee it is apparent that the hegemony the ruling politicians wield over the public servants enables and facilitates TCOs' enterprises in Belize. In addition, the domination of the state infrastructure by the ruling politicians in a structure of government patterned on the United Kingdom model facilitates the quest for hegemony over the contested spaces of the Belizean social order by TCOs. The hegemony of ruling politicians over the agencies of the state create malformed state institutions incapable of formulating and applying the mechanisms and apparatuses of power necessary to dominating the spaces in the social order. Hegemonic politicians are only interested in their political hegemony expressed via victory at the polls and a pliant population until the next election. To attain this end, you utilise political instruments forged under colonial domination now married to mass voter mobilisation. Central to this is the use of the national security apparatus primarily the police to police political dissent and unrest. In Belize there is then no mechanism to ensure power relations are managed to ensure that individuals of the social order are dominated, docile and disciplined through policing themselves which is demanded by the model of government in place as of independence from colonial domination. Contested spaces are produced by this malformed state where without the need for working alliances with the ruling politicians and the agents of the state the TCOs of Belize entered, now dominate and are expanding the expanse of these spaces in the Belizean geography. To this reality must now be incorporated the operational alliances between the TCOs, ruling politicians of Belize and agents of the state/public servants of the state of Belize within agencies and spaces of the state. Compromised spaces of the Belizean state are all encompassing including the security apparatus which is tactically necessary as TCOs view this as simply buying insurance to cover the expected betrayal of politicians. The aim is to attain a position of dominance where ruling politicians are moved to do nothing relevant and meaningful in spite of political pressure both local and international. To do this you exert hegemony over the oligarchs of the social order as the politicians are subservient to the oligarchs at the level of the idea hence worldview. Whilst the politicians are already immersed in the power relations of the illicit enterprises of the TCOs effectively silencing those who are not. These power relations then constitute bi-polar actors of the state agencies and political realm as they straddle two realms that are supposedly anathema to each other: the lawful, licit/illicit, illegal, the sacred and the profane. Which is reflected in the individuals and the nature of human action in the social order.

Belize is now integrated into the trafficking networks of the TCOs present in Belize especially the MTTOs as a result of these dire failings of the government model adopted with independence. The state form cobbled together and transplanted/grafted to/on a colonial social order alien to its genesis and devoid of the discursive apparatuses necessary to drive this state form has resulted in the evolution of a Frankenstein monster in Belize. But this gravely bi-polar state form is evolving under the impact of the alliance between TCOs, the ruling politicians and the agencies of the state with a model already in existence that is illustrative of one possible evolutionary path in the Caribbean basin i.e. the Dominican Republic.

The discourse of corruption commonly utilised in the Caribbean to explain the failure of the state and the politicians to effectively deal with the impact of TCOs on the social order of Caribbean states cannot explain this complex reality. This discourse cannot recognise the malaise of a state form that evolved in a European context being copied and transplanted on a social order that has not evolved the necessary discursive apparatuses to drive this state form and never will. The state form transplanted in its malformed and dysfunctional operational condition cannot exercise the hegemony it demands over the power relations of the social order. The reality is that the power relations coupled to this externally imposed state form are not produced by the social order it was grafted onto. It's not then humans being corrupt but the state being incapable to exert hegemony over the power relations thrown up by the social order hence the endemic gun violence. The discourse of corruption is but another mask peddled by the politicians, academia and others for failure to see and admit the underlying reality. This is not a case of a failed state for the state form imposed never functioned much less to fail. Sovereignty and law was never hegemonic much less for us to become lawless. International power relations after independence was the first potent reality that illustrated the weakness of the state caused by arrested development. The second was the fracturing off the social order by the discourses of voter mobilisation utilised by the politicians and the present potent reality of the assault of TCOs and their alternate social order beckons to a new bi-polar social order rooted in the operational existence of a licit and illicit social order and the boundary along which they interact and rub up against each other with the humans that traverse these perceptual and discursive domains in tow. Simply living in Hell!

CHAPTER 3
The Terrain of Organised Crime

There are three major trafficking transition zones in Belize: the border zone with Guatemala, the border zone with Mexico and the border zone with the Caribbean Sea which includes the seaport of Belize City. The international airport as the seaport serves the transnational trafficking organisations of Belize. Cocaine hydrochloride kilo bricks enter Belize via the port, airport, illicit landing strips and illicit entry points on the Caribbean coastline and are moved into Mexico and Guatemala. This movement has necessitated the creation of the three transition zones where the hegemony of the state is challenged or absent on the ground. There is a counter movement of kilo bricks exported from Belize to the Caribbean island chain and consumer markets of the North Atlantic via diverse means as containerised cargo, swallowers, mules, fishing vessels, general cargo etc. Then there is the local drug market supplied with cocaine for wholesale and retail sales. The importation of precursors for the manufacture of synthetic drugs then moved to Mexico and Guatemala to methamphetamine labs is another strategic task assigned to the operations of transnational crime in Belize. These is also the trafficking of methamphetamine from Belize into Mexico as the availability of the industrial grade meth produced by the Mexican Transnational Trafficking Organisations (MTTOs) has created a secondary meth trafficking stream involving Belize and Belizean nationals in Mexico. Meth is as a result available for export on Belizean drug markets as it now flows along the illicit drug arteries of CARICOM and other islands of the Caribbean. Heroin whether produced in Mexico, Colombia, Honduras or elsewhere enters Belize and is trafficked via Belize on its way to the crossing points along the Mexico-US border or via the Caribbean island chain to North-East USA.

Belize is then an operational asset in the premier drug matrix of the MTTOs for the Western Hemisphere: meth, heroin and cocaine. This strategic position demands a level of engagement with the ruling politicians and the agents of the state as illustrated by the audit report of the IND and other revelations that have emerged. In addition, this strategic importance as an operational asset raises questions on the integrity of the security agencies of the state as the MTTOs in their strategic plan to secure their operations invest heavily in subverting the military and the police of states as Belize. Furthermore, the MTTOs in countries as Belize implement the strategy of creating manufacturing facilities for their premier product matrix. Coca paste is trafficked to manufacturing facilities in these countries and turned into cocaine hydrochloride and precursors imported into these countries are fed into meth labs in these countries with the product then trafficked to the next staging area in the trafficking pipeline. Are there cocaine and meth labs presently operating in Belize under the control of the MTTOs and their gangland affiliates? The same process can also be applied to heroin production where the opium paste is carried to labs in countries where the precursors are easily available. The border transition zones with Guatemala and Mexico are the expected areas where these labs can be situated but this reality also applies to Belize City just as well. The second tier of illicit drugs consists of marijuana/ganja and other synthetic drugs as MDMA/ecstasy and the rapidly rising fentanyl. The drug of choice on the drug markets of Belize is ganja with the predominant issue being supply to match demand especially in the Belize City drug market and the production and trafficking of high potency organic ganja to the US North-East. The ganja market significantly contributes to the gang violence of Belize City especially Southside more so than the premier drug matrix. The primary driving issue on the local ganja market is matching supply to demand as demand presently outstrips supply which gives rise to the dynamic of which group dominates supply and the most profitable retail turf. On the supply side imports and home grown product are sought as solutions to supply side shortfalls but the range of imports from a range of supply points external of Belize points to the regional ganja dynamic unleashed by the MTTOs and their Caribbean gangland affiliates. This dynamic aims at maximising the production of high potency organic ganja that fetches premium prices on the wholesale ganja markets of the US North-East especially New York City which impacts the level of supply of plantation grade ganja which contributes to the ganja wars of the Caribbean basin. Which is enhanced by the trafficking of premium ganja from the Caribbean basin as predators who are intent on seizing the product from trafficking cells escalate the levels of graphic tit for tat violence on the ground. This is a market where the impact of the strategy of the MTTOs and their Caribbean gangland affiliates has shattered the rules of the game that existed before their rise to hegemony. The centrality of the ganja market in the terrain of gang violence in Southside, Belize City was illustrated in a statement to the press by Senior Superintendent Marco Vidal Commander of the Southside Police, Belize City in September 2017 reported on Amandala.com. In response to a reporter's question Vidal said: "The reporter's question: "Are you alluding to the widely held perception that certain groups were allowed to thrive in the marijuana trade while others were not allowed to thrive on that trade under the previous commander?" Vidal answered: "Exactly, and obviously, you have your information from that world." The reporter replied: "I said it was a perception." Vidal replied: "I don't know if it was a perception. I'm sure you have your sources there and you would know that there was some perception, if you may, that there were some persons allowed to do some things and others not allowed to do the same thing. My position is and my strategy is that it is across the board. You commit an offense, and you will face the consequences for that offense." Vidal is insisting that the joint enterprise between specific Southside, Belize City gangs and the Southside police has distorted the ganja drug market and the balance of power among the gangs of Southside. The nature of the market intervention by the Southside police will feed a gang war in Southside seen in the murder rate for 2017. Vidal's position is that the much touted gang truce of Southside before his arrival at the Southside police did not result in or ensure gangland peace as the basis for a bloody long term gang war in Southside was laid during the period of selective policing/market intervention which manifested itself in the number of murders in 2017 in Southside and this trend continued into 2018. This then is the present Belizean ganja wars. It's also a potent lesson on the impact the illicit joint enterprise between organised crime and agents of the state will have on the social order especially on the level of gun violence in the social order. The 7newsbelize.com news report for March 16, 2018 reported that Senior Superintendent Marco Vidal was removed as Commander of Southside command and re-assigned to the Special Branch of the BPD. Marco Vidal was replaced at Southside command by Senior Superintendent Howell Gillet. Assistant Commissioner of Police Chester Williams who was replaced by Marco Vidal at Southside was named as Deputy Commissioner of Police in charge of Operations

http://amandala.com.bz/news/marco-takes-chester/

http://www.7newsbelize.com/sstory.php?nid=44049

http://amandala.com.bz/news/police-department-shakeup/

The synthetic drugs of the second tier will be trafficked in tablet and or liquid form along the pipelines used for meth precursors and meth trafficking. In other strategic drug transition zones of the Caribbean basin the manufacture of fentanyl from imported raw materials has commenced as in the Dominican Republic this then is the possible next stage for Belize.

Instances of Trafficking

Drug Flights

Indicators of this trade that appeared in the media of Belize are as follows: the discovery of light aircraft intact and abandoned or destroyed in Orange Walk close to the border with Mexico. The discovery of two burnt light aircraft in the transition zone with Mexico one at Orange Walk between Indian Church and Hill Bank reported on February 26th,2018 and the other at the Corozal District in the Santa Cruz area of Libertad Village reported on February 27th 2018 on 7belizenews.com. A King Air Beechcraft 200 was found abandoned in north western Belize close to the Belize-Mexico border as reported in a 7newsbelize.com news report of March 15, 2018. A 7newsbelize.com report of April 13, 2018 stated that an illicit plane entered, landed and took off from the broad area of between mile 10 of the George Price Highway and the Coastal Road perhaps all the way to La Democracia in the Belize district in spite of the police response to the area.

These reports indicate that the MTTOs have now increased the volume of drug flights into Belize in 2018 where the transition zone of Belize with Mexico will become a holding and transition zone of note and importance for moving product into Mexico. This is an indication of the hegemony the MTTOs now exert over the social order and the state of Belize with the telling impact of this hegemony on the nature of the social order destined to rapidly evolve. The frequency of these discoveries of illicit aircraft in Belize now raise the question of the actual volume of flights undetected which questions the efficacy of the national security apparatus of Belize?

http://www.reporter.bz/front-page/suspected-drug-plane-lands-in-belize/

http://amandala.com.bz/news/plane-destroyed-suspected-drug-plane/

http://www.reporter.bz/crime/drug-plane-found-burnt-in-corn-field/

http://www.7newsbelize.com/sstory.php?nid=43839

http://www.7newsbelize.com/sstory.php?nid=43857

http://www.7newsbelize.com/sstory.php?nid=44035

http://www.7newsbelize.com/sstory.php?nid=44375

The smuggling of cocaine into Belize from Mexico and the smuggling of cocaine from Belize into Mexico via the border crossing at the Northern Border, Corozal, Belize. The cocaine smuggled into Belize was interdicted and found to carry one of the brands of the MTTOs.

http://www.reporter.bz/front-page/police-seize-315000-worth-of-cocaine/

http://amandala.com.bz/news/suv-crashed-abandoned-6328-grams-cocaine-northern-border/

http://www.reporter.bz/crime/cocaine-smuggler-leaves-drugs-behind-flees-for-freedom/

http://amandala.com.bz/news/mexican-marines-nab-3-belizeans/

The trafficking of heroin between Belize and Mexico again via the Northern Border:

http://amandala.com.bz/news/2-4-million-heroin-bust-corozal/

http://www.reporter.bz/front-page/cops-seize-heroin-worth-10000000-drugs-have-suspicious-links-to-nigeria-destined-for-north-america/

http://amandala.com.bz/news/3-men-woman-remanded-16-5-pounds-heroin/

The trafficking of crystal meth and its precursors between Belize and Mexico via the Northern Border:

http://amandala.com.bz/news/2-jailed-crystal-meth-worth-bz4-million/

http://amandala.com.bz/news/mexicans-release-nortenos-nabbed-45-kilo-crystal-meth-bust/

http://amandala.com.bz/news/suspected-crystal-meth-precursor-chemicals-discovered-bullet-tree/

http://amandala.com.bz/news/crystal-meth-precursors-seized-mexico/

The local growth and production of ganja and an idea of the volume of the Belizean ganja trade is indicated by the following:

http://www.reporter.bz/weekend-news/police-make-weekend-drug-seizures/

http://www.reporter.bz/weekend-news/drug-trafficking-and-customs-bust-in-guinea-grass/

http://www.reporter.bz/crime/gsu-find-51-pounds-of-weed-in-western-paradise/

Gangland and Illicit Firearms

The light weapons trade continues to impact the Caribbean basin and Belize is no exception seen in its gang wars especially in Belize City. An illicit trade that exploded in expanse and volume under Colombian traffickers is now undergoing deep seated change under the hegemony of the MTTOs and their gangland affiliates. The MTTOs and their extensive light weapons acquisition and trafficking structures of the USA has enhanced the light weapons trafficking capacity of their Caribbean gangland affiliates with an operational presence in the USA. This has resulted in the marked increase in the volume and types of light weapons sourced in and smuggled from the USA in the hands of Caribbean gangland presently. This has sparked an arms race in Caribbean gangland as the affiliates of the MTTOs brandishing their acquired USA firepower with the required level of supply and possession to dominate gangland has forced those locked out of this special relationship with the MTTOs to seek the same and comparative firepower by any means necessary. This arms race is summed up in the power the possession of and the powerlessness the non-possession of the AR15 assault rifle now bestows in Caribbean gangland. The supply of illicit firearms to Belize is diverse as smuggled weapons enter via all the transition zones especially the transition zones with Mexico and Guatemala.

The gangland militias of the MTTOs in the transition zones of Belize are charged with maintaining the operational environment of these zones for the traffickers of the MTTOs. This is an illicit operation and its premised on the use of illicit violence to ensure the hegemony of the social order thrown up by the illicit enterprises of the transition zones. The monopoly of violence that only the state enjoys under the discourse of sovereignty in these zones is then under constant assault. The illicit arms trade weaponises the social order which is a deliberate strategy in the assault on the hegemony of the state. This is then an illicit business in the service of the premier business model of drug trafficking. It's obvious in Belize that the strategy is played out in the gun violence of specific spaces of Belize City (Southside) which is an ongoing political issue with the gaze of the state fixed on these urban spaces whilst the premier transition zones and the illicit activities of these zones namely the zones with Mexico and Guatemala are fleeting political issues as they command the interest of the state in short bursts at best.

Gangland Belize is diverse comprising the following groups: the gangs/militias of the border zones dominated by Mexican organisations and their gangland affiliates, the gangs of the Caribbean Sea transition zone who are affiliates of the MTTOs and those who are not affiliates. Those not affiliated to the MTTOs as a result are being increasingly marginalised from the trafficking enterprise such as specific gangs in Southside Belize City. Then there are the transnational gangland sets which belong to US national and transnational gangs comprising Belizeans and those of Belizean origin and ethnicity. These sets form part of gangs who are affiliated to the MTTOs, are part of the MTTOs trafficking infrastructure of the USA and are now operating in Belize as part of the trafficking infrastructure of the MTTOs that links Belize to the USA, Canada, Europe, West Africa, Brazil and the Caribbean island chain. Sets of the Los Angeles Crips and Bloods dominated by ethnic Belizeans are the most potent examples of this reality in Belize. What is noteworthy in sets of the Crips and Bloods in Belize is the blending of Caribbean gangland culture and methodology with that of LA Crips and Bloods official gang culture to form a hybrid set where members will not wear ink, colours nor represent but will defend the set with their lives whilst others will express the official Crips and Bloods patterns of gang behaviour. Internecine warfare within and between sets is also present in Belize.

https://www.youtube.com/watch?v=Bv3XzVJk5nQ

Gangland of Southside, Belize City is not then representative of gangland Belize. Within Southside there are gangs affiliated to affiliates of the MTTOs or to the MTTOs themselves juxtaposed with those who don't enjoy such links but control space. The gangland structure of Southside was established during the era of the hegemony of Colombian traffickers where the Mexican traffickers were employees of the Colombians. The Caribbean coastline and its proximity to the port of Belize City created Southside as an operational hub during the Colombian era. The rise of the Valle Norte organisation in the decade of the 1990s with its new business model resulted in the growing power of the Mexican traffickers in Belize but this was also the period when Belizean traffickers with access purchased kilo bricks and became traffickers, wholesalers and retailers in their own right. During the hegemony of this business model the gun violence in Southside exploded as an internecine war for turf, kilos, guns and income driven by tit for tat killings generated a self-perpetuating momentum of its own. The exertion of MTTOs hegemony over trafficking in Belize and the Caribbean basin during the late 1990s and the first decade of the 21st century set in train the rolling out on the ground of a new business model that rejected the Valle Norte organisation's model with a return to the principles of the Medellin and Cali organisations model but now structured with an emphasis on integration, globalisation and rigidly policed discipline. The MTTOs rigorously apply the dictum in operational zones where hegemony is exercised that the products of the organisation are circulated only within the organisation and with its partners, affiliates and the affiliates of its partners and affiliates. This simply means that in drug markets where this structure operates in their products are not wholesaled outside of this umbrella organisational structure. In Southside there are then haves and have nots with gangs connected to the umbrella organisation of the MTTOs evolving into traffickers within the organisation, possessing light weapons in quality and quantity that change the strategic terrain and the balance of power and most importantly their wealth generation now places them in the ranks of globalised players. Whilst those excluded are faced with marginalisation and decimation which feeds a desperate feeding frenzy noted for graphic violence devoid of strategic intent. This is a long term engagement as indicated by the reality of Gangland Jamaica as it in no way hinders the hegemony of the MTTOs nor does it negatively impact the profit maximisation drive of the illicit enterprises of the MTTOs. The illicit enterprises prosper in spite of the internecine warfare which indicates the political purpose served by the warfare as it impacts the social order as an alternate order rooted in illicit activity seizes control in specific spaces. Whilst the state resorts to counter insurgency inspired measures with its military discourse as "suppression" which cannot end the internecine war nor dismantle the illicit enterprises of the said spaces. The state simply concedes hegemony of these spaces to the MTTOs.

Murders Belize

Gangland Belize is therefore showing all the signs of a mature gang landscape driven by the strategic agenda of the MTTOs. This gangland reality especially that of Southside, Belize City is reflected in the annual total of murders for Belize in the 21st century especially during the period 2012 to 2017 with 2012 having the highest number of murders in the history of Belize-145 and 2017 second with 142. Clearly, from 2002 with 64 murders the annual murder count rose to a level which it has never yet fallen below and continued rising peaking in 2012 with 145 murders and again in 2017 with 142 murders. The base for the new normal was set in 2009 when for the first time the murder count crossed 100 with 103 murders. The evolution of the annual murder count must then be juxtaposed to the evolution of the illicit trades of Belize in its globalised context in order to gain insights as to the realities of the illicit trades that impact the level of violence in the social order. This is exhibited in the

evolution of the murder rate of Belize from the 1990s to the 21st century. In 1993 the murder rate was 24 per 100,000 persons in 1995 it was 28 per 100,000 persons but in the period 1993 to 1999 it was only in 1998 that the murder rate per 100,000 fell below 20 per 100,000 with 16 per 100,000. For the period 1993 to 1999 the rate moved from a low of 20 per 100,000 to a high of 28 per 100,000. In 2000 the murder rate was 16 per 100,000 persons and in 2001 it was 25 per 100,000 persons but from 2002 it rose to 33 per 100,000 persons whilst in 2003, 2004 and 2005 the murder rate was 24, 28 and 28 per 100,000 persons respectively. In 2006 the murder rate was 30 per 100,000 persons and from 2006 to 2017 it was only in 2013 the murder rate fell out of the thirties to 28 per 100,000 persons. In 2008 the murder rate was 33 per 100,000, in 2010 it rose to 40 per 100,000 persons for the first time peaking in 2012 at 43 per 100,000 persons and in 2016 and 2017 falling to 37 per 100,000 persons for each year. In the 1990s it was already high reflecting the Colombian transnational trafficking organisations business model and the violence that ensued especially when the model collapsed. From

the 21st century with the rise in dominance of the MTTOs eventually attaining hegemony where the new business model is now impacting Gangland Belize the result is a heightened level of violence. The murder rate peak in 2010 of 40 per 100,000 persons appeared literally out of nowhere as the rate for the preceding years were all below 35 per 100,000 and these were the years of the collapse of the hegemonic Colombian traffickers and the rolling out of the agenda of the MTTOs with a change of personnel, business model and order on the ground which impacted Gangland Belize. From the peak of 2010 the motion was set in train with the peak of 2012 now feeding the development and evolution of a new reality in the Belizean social order not only in gangland which is the new normal of the murder spiral. From 2014 to 2017 the murder rate has been climbing in the thirties range over a period of four years if this continues in 2018 then the new normal is in place where a murder rate in the high thirties and low forties will be common per year constituting the new normal.

The OSAC Belize 2018 Crime and Safety Report states that in 2017 some 58% of murders were by the gun. The 2017 murder rate for Belize City was 90 per 100,000. For 2017 the distribution of murders by district was as follows: Belize: 82 murders (57.74%), Cayo: 28 murders (19.71%), Orange Walk: 9 murders (6.33%), Stann Creek: 12 murders (8.45%), Corozal: 8 murders (5.63%) and Toledo: 3 murders (2.11 %) Total=142. For 2016 the total murders were 138 with Belize district recording 70 (50.72%) and Cayo district 34 (26.81%). In 2016 82 murders were by firearms (59.42%). In 2015 the total murders were 119 with Belize district recording 66 (55.46%) and Cayo district 27 (22.68%). In 2015 71 murders were by firearms (59.66%). The murder rate of Belize is then directly linked to the gangland reality on the ground in Belize district especially in the contested spaces of gangland Belize City particularly Southside, Belize City. And for 2015 to 2017 the gun accounts for over 50% of the total murders recorded for Belize on an annual basis. Belize's murder landscape is then directly linked to illicit small arms and ammunition smuggling that feeds the gang wars of particularly Belize City.

http://www.reporter.bz/business/belize-just-ended-its-2nd-most-murderous-year-in-history/

https://www.osac.gov/pages/ContentReportDetails.aspx?cid=23360

http://www.oas.org/dsp/Observatorio/database/countriesdetails.aspx?lang=en&country=BLZ

Human Smuggling

The most lucrative and globalised illicit enterprise in Belize is human smuggling particularly the flow through Belize into Mexico on the way to the USA and Canada which is under the hegemony of the MTTOs. The human smuggling pipelines that operate in Belize are diverse seen in the flows and the transnational organised crime groups present in Belize. The pipelines are: The East Asian flow moving Chinese from the People's Republic of China and Taiwan. Chinese moving along this pipeline enter Belize on their way to

Mexico for entry to the US and Canada. Other Chinese enter Belize to settle there as a holding area until they move on to various other destinations within the Caribbean basin whilst others settle in Belize permanently. As a result of this Chinese flow the snake heads of the People's Republic of China especially those of Fujianese organised crime and the dragon tails of the Triads of Taiwan are present in Belize with the Triads arriving under British colonial rule. It must be noted that the human smuggling operations of Sister Ping to New York was a Fujianese organised operation that involved their presence in Belize. The Snake Heads of Fujian organised crime are the most noted of human smuggling organised crime in the west but they are not the only transnational organised crime (TOC) groups out of China operating in the Caribbean basin. In the Caribbean basin they are the hegemonic Chinese TOC group as in the case of Belize.

The Case of Sister Ping or Chen Chiu Ping or Xiu Qing Zhang or Lily Zhang

With the debacle of the sea vessel Golden Venture in 1993 running aground on the coast of Queens borough, New York City with some 286 illegal immigrants on board Sister Ping and her various aliases became the subject of an international manhunt. What was subsequently discovered was: Sister Ping had in her possession a Belizean passport when she was arrested in Hong Kong in 2000 and extradited to the USA in 2003. And Sister Ping and the Fujianese transnational organised crime group of the People's Republic of China she was part of smuggled Chinese immigrants into Belize, to Mexico then to the US and Canada. Checks in Belize revealed that in May 1988 a passport was issued to Xiu Qing Zhang and some twelve years later or in 2000 a new passport was issued to Xing Qing Zhang under the name of Lily Zhang. It was determined that Xiu Qing Zhang purchased her passport under the original Economic Citizenship Programme. Acquiring a Belizean passport was strategically necessary to Sister Ping's allotted task in the Fujianese organised crime organisation as a Snake Head charged with the responsibility of managing all aspects of a pipeline moving illicit immigrants from China to the USA and Canada. As in the decade of the 1980s Sister Ping was an active operative involved in establishing the human smuggling pipeline from China to the USA under the control of Fujianese organised crime. Belize was one entry point on the journey to Mexico then to the USA and Canada which meant that an organised crime infrastructure with its operatives was put in place and maintained in Belize. This operational presence was managed by Sister Ping and she answered to the command of the crime group for its affairs. Which meant that Sister Ping availed herself of the opportunity to purchase a Belizean passport according to the economic citizenship programme. In the aftermath of the Golden Venture fiasco it is highly likely that Sister Ping visited Belize in the course of her duties to the organised crime group. And the infrastructure of the Fujianese transnational organised crime group expanded and further developed by Sister Ping in Belize exists to this day with their operatives being part of the organised crime enterprise in the IND. Fujianese organised crime in conjunction with other organised crime groups of the People's Republic of China along with the Triads are operationally present in Belize.

http://edition.channel5belize.com/archives/11534

http://edition.channel5belize.com/archives/11528

https://www.nytimes.com/2014/04/28/nyregion/cheng-chui-ping-a-smuggler-of-immigrants-dies-in-prison-but-is-praised-in-chinatown.html

https://www.newyorker.com/magazine/2006/04/24/the-snakehead

The South Asian flow from India, Bangladesh and Sri Lanka where families and clans utilise local human smuggling organised crime groups who are linked to the coyotes of the MTTOs for the trip via Mexico to the US and Canada. Family ties are used to enter and settle in Belize temporarily until arrangements are made with coyotes in Belize for the onward trip, to settle permanently in Belize or to move around the Caribbean basin. The North Asian flow from Pakistan, Afghanistan and Nepal where the local networks linked to the coyotes sell complete packages to clients. The links to the coyotes of the MTTOs in this region are quite established and vibrant especially in Afghanistan and Pakistan. The Latin American/Caribbean flow has the largest volume comprising migrants from Central, South America and the Caribbean who utilise Belize as their entry point to Mexico on their way to the Mexico-US border. This flow is under the hegemony of the MTTOs and it's the traditional mainstay of the human smuggling enterprise of Mexican organised crime. The MTTOs have applied various strategies to increase the volume of its clientele for this service by utilising various push discourses to convince prospective clients around the world that entering the US or Canada is affordable, possible and available. This is seen in the launch of the Eastern Europe and Balkans flow where clients from these areas are now entering the Caribbean as illicit migrants as in the Dominican Republic and amongst them are those on their way to the Mexico-US border where Belize is but another stop over.

The MTTOs then clearly exercise hegemony over the human smuggling enterprise of Belize and other TOC groups present in Belize have an alliance with the MTTOs which covers a range of other illicit activities. Through this link with Chinese organised crime doors are open to the Chinese markets for MTTOs' products and the Chinese TOC groups also traffic illicit products to China and from China to the Caribbean. The pipeline from the Caribbean to China is then a dual flow pipeline where illicit drugs, gold, coltan, high value animal parts as fish bladders and turtle shells and exotic species many endangered move to China. From Belize specifically there are the prized rosewood lumber, sea cucumbers, queen conch, lobsters and wildlife as howler and spider monkeys, the scarlet headed macaw, the yellow headed parrot and the hicatee turtle. Whilst synthetic drugs precursors synthetic drugs as fentanyl, knock offs/counterfeit goods flow from China. The demand for the species of rosewood in Belize (Dalbergia stevensoni) is in great demand making it one of the hottest trafficked products in the world since 2013 seen in the exports to satisfy the level of demand in China. The stands of rosewood in Belize have been decimated by illicit logging that feeds international trafficking raising questions on the prospect of the survival of the species in Belize. Decimation of the stands of rosewood in the Toledo and Stann Creek regions of Belize is linked to the transition zone of the Western border with Belize and Guatemala and to organised crime in Belize. In 2012 the government of Belize placed a moratorium on the harvesting of rosewood and in 2013 rosewood was added to the regulated list of items of CITES which means that exports of rosewood from Belize have to be certified that they were harvested legally and sustainably. In spite of the moratorium and the CITES designation rosewood stands continue to be plundered on private and public lands. The plunder of the rosewood stock is only feasible if they are monetised and to do so they must be exported which means that various mechanisms are in place which allow the export of illicit Belizean rosewood. This is done directly through the Belizean port with the complicity of agents of the state and via Guatemala where stolen Belizean rosewood is smuggled through the western border transition zone into Guatemala for export. Or stolen Belizean rosewood is moved into Guatemala then exported to Belize for export as legal Guatemalan rosewood with the necessary Guatemalan documentation. The entire rosewood smuggling operation of Belize is linked to organised crime and an illicit enterprise involving transnational organised crime and agents of the state. The vital links to Guatemalan operations and the involvement of Guatemalan nationals at all level of the illicit rosewood trade in Belize indicate the involvement of the MTTOs working in conjunction with their Chinese TOC partners. In the aftermath of the March 2013 decision of CITES to list rosewood the Government of Belize declared an amnesty on the sale of rosewood from April 8 to 26, 2013 solely to the government. All stock of seized rosewood in the custody of the government was released to the government and persons holding stock were invited to surrender their stock to the government during the period of amnesty. The government sold the stock collected to a Belizean company owned by German Ignacio Vega brother of then Minister of Lands, Gaspar Vega for B$ 5 per board foot when the going rates on the international market ranges between USD10 to USD15 per board foot. Gaspar Vega then sold the stock of rosewood on the international market excluding China according to the government. It's expected that German Vega continues to be at present one of the largest legal traders of rosewood in Belize. The terrain of the politicisation of the Belizean social order is again apparent.

http://amandala.com.bz/news/china-hot-for-toledo-rosewood-ngos-warn-of-rapid-depletion/

http://amandala.com.bz/news/big-rosewood-bust-benque/

http://amandala.com.bz/news/rosewood-hot-5-busted/

http://amandala.com.bz/news/rosewood-inventory-exposes-threat-stock-decimation/

http://amandala.com.bz/news/cabinet-orders-confiscated-rosewood-sold-german-vega/

http://www.reporter.bz/features/we-stand-for-wildlife-tackling-the-illegal-trade-in-belize/

An example of human smuggling in Belize utilising the coyotes of the MTTOs with undocumented Guatemalans and US dollars in cash being smuggled:

http://www.reporter.bz/crime/authorities-foil-suspected-human-trafficking-attempt/

An example of the operation of organised crime involved in human smuggling through Belize to Mexico of Hondurans. The seven adults and eight children reportedly entered Belize illicitly from Guatemala and were being transported towards the border with Mexico when interdicted. What is noteworthy in this instance is the number of children being smuggled.

http://www.7newsbelize.com/sstory.php?nid=44341

The 2010 Housing and Population Census of Belize presents a breakdown of the foreign born population of Belize by nationality of origin which places in context the impact of human smuggling on the social order of Belize. Between the 2000 and 2010 censuses the foreign born population grew by 19.9 % from 36,642 persons in 2000 to 45,723 in 2010 holding steady at 14% of national population. Distribution of the foreign population in Belize shows 32.9% living in the Cayo district and 25.2% live in the Belize district. By nationality of origin Guatemala accounts for 42.5% of the total foreign born population in 2000 and 41.3% in 2010. Followed by El Salvador with 17.7% in 2000 and 15.5% in 2010 and Honduras with 14.5% in 2000 and 15.3% in 2010. In the period Honduras has overtaken El Salvador for the second largest supplier of migrants. It is apparent from the 2010 census that Salvadorians, Hondurans and Guatemalans are using Belize as a transition zone to Mexico especially in the case of the Salvadorians and the Hondurans as Guatemala has a border with Mexico. From the census information Nicaraguan migration has increased from 0.8% in 2000 to 1.4% in 2010 indicating the growth and expansion of pipelines into the human smuggling transition zone of Belize from points external of Belize. The fall in Mexican migration from 6.8% in 2000 to 4.9% in 2010 reflects the changing reality on the ground in Belize as the MTTOs exert their hegemony. Whilst migration from the USA increased from 5.1% in 2000 to 6.2 % in 2010 which reflects the return flow of those born in the USA of the Belizean Diaspora including those involved in the illicit trades. China in 2000 accounted for 4.6% of the foreign born population and 3.8% in 2010 whilst India in 2000 accounted for 0.8% and 1.1% in 2010 which means that Indian migration to Belize is growing illustrating the expansion of the source market for migration to Belize and the constancy of flow from China to Belize. The category Other in 2000 was 5.8% of foreign born population and 8.5% in 2010 which means that there is a multiplicity of nationalities heading to Belize in trickles which amounts to a growing portion of the foreign born population of Belize. In 2000 it was ranked 5th in the line-up and in 2010 it was now 4th. The data then presents the dominant source markets for human smuggling to Belize, the nature of the flow of nationalities through the Belize transition zone and members of these nationalities that have settled in Belize. From within the communities of nationalities settled in Belize the infrastructure of human smuggling is located for migrants of those nationalities. This movement of migrants is then the basis for the organised crime enterprise of the IND which is the sale of state issued immigration and nationality documents.

http://sib.org.bz/wp-content/uploads/2017/05/Census_Report_2010.pdf

Evasion of Customs duties and taxes

The smuggling of alcohol products, cigarettes, foodstuff, pharmaceuticals and fuel to evade taxes and Customs duties for sale on the Belizean and other national markets via Belize is a common illicit activity in Belize. This is especially so through the northern border with Mexico via the Free Trade Zone that straddles the borders of Mexico and Belize. The smuggling of fuel stolen in Mexico to energy poor nations of Central America is part of the illicit fuel smuggling enterprise of Mexican organised crime that ensures the supply of fuel necessary to trafficking pipelines in keeping with the principle of fail-safe systems in trafficking structures.

Counterfeit pharmaceuticals

The Belize Ministry of Health issued an advisory on an "unauthorised and suspected falsified" vitamin and mineral supplement as the product "has not been registered by the Ministry and therefore cannot be imported into the country as it has not met the necessary quality standards and may be compromised." The advisory of the Ministry of Health recognises the existence of the trade in illicit pharmaceuticals when it stated: "The public is advised…to abstain from purchasing products from unlicensed or unauthorised establishments and peddlers." According to the 7newsbelize.com news report this was possibly a case of a counterfeit from Guatemala of a Mexican product.

http://www.7newsbelize.com/sstory.php?nid=43999

Organised crime cigarette smuggling between Belize and Guatemala and beyond was interdicted and smuggling for sale on the Belizean market via the Northern Border is common.

http://amandala.com.bz/news/cigarette-ring-busted-guatemala-roots-belize/

http://www.reporter.bz/front-page/guatemalans-say-contraband-cigarettes-originated-in-belize/

http://www.reporter.bz/general/joint-police-operation-yields-contraband-cigarettes/

The smuggling of ganja and other illicit drugs with contraband goods to evade Customs duties and taxes is a strategy in Belize.

http://www.reporter.bz/weekend-news/drug-trafficking-and-customs-bust-in-guinea-grass/

The smuggling of ganja and ammunition from Mexico into Belize.

In a news report dated April 6, 2018 on reporter.bz four residents of Hattieville, Belize were arrested at the Belize-Mexico border with 58.5 pounds of ganja in the spare tyres of two vehicles and 28 rounds of .380 calibre ammunition in the spare tyre of one vehicle on April 4, 2018. Both vehicles and the four occupants travelled from Belize to Chetumal Quinta Roo, Mexico and were interdicted on their way back to Belize.

http://www.reporter.bz/weekend-news/authorities-confiscate-drugs-and-ammo-at-mexican-border/

Money Laundering

The business model of the MTTOs generates loads of cash in the consumer nations that must be washed and placed in circulation within the international financial order. Loads of cash in USDs are moved out of the US to transition zones where the washing commences but entry into circulation within the international financial order demands delivery of the hard physical cash at some point in the process. Caribbean island offshore financial centres and offshore financial centres of non-island countries of the Caribbean basin are strategic players in this laundry. Belize is part of this Caribbean basin transition zone with the volume of activity through Belize determined by the quality of the services available in Belize, its linkages to the offshore financial centres and the international financial order and the present operational strategy of the money laundering cells of the MTTOs.

An extradition request from the USA for the Belize based attorney Andrew Bennett has placed in the public domain the Puerto Rico grand jury indictment dated July 2015 of Bennett on 7 counts of money laundering the proceeds of drug traffickers via international banks operating in Belize. Approached by an undercover DEA agent the indictment states that Bennet agreed to launder the proceeds of drug trafficking for a Colombian and a Puerto Rican trafficking organisation. Bennett was subsequently handed USD 250,000 by the undercover agent in Belize which he accepted as dirty drug money in need of washing according to the indictment. The indictment states that Bennett subsequently washed the dirty money placing the proceeds in accounts in Atlanta, Georgia, USA, in New York City, New York, USA and in Puerto Rico less 20% of the sum of money washed which was his fee for services rendered. Bennett is presently out on bail granted in the Magistrates' Courts at the arraignment arising from the US extradition request.

http://www.7newsbelize.com/sstory.php?nid=43177&frmsrch=1

http://www.7newsbelize.com/sstory.php?nid=43401&frmsrch=1

The level of operational activity of transnational organised crime in Belize then demands a working relationship with the ruling politicians and the agencies of the state. This then places the state form of Belize under grave scrutiny and pressure exerted by TOC groups whose resources at hand outstrip those of the Belizean state. This state form has then to respond to this assault but its ability to react in the manner strategically necessary to preserve its sovereignty is determined by its power relations arising from its operational discourses. A state form that is discordant, malformed and underdeveloped easily capitulates. It's then much more than the corruption of politicians and agencies of the state as it's an organic problem.

The INCSRs of the US State Department

The International Narcotics Control Strategy Report INCSR) prepared by and published in the public domain by the US State Department provides a glimpse of the geopolitics of the war on drugs and the policing of money laundering by the US and the discourses utilised by the State Department. This study will analyse the reports for the years 2018, 2017 and 2016 which are the reports for the years 2017, 2016 and 2015 respectively. In the 2018 Volume 1 report on Belize in Section B. 4 which deals with corruption the report states: "A Special Audit of the Immigration and Nationality Department found multiple cases of fraud and corruption within the department." What then is the reason the State Department gives for such corruption? The report states at Section B. 4: "However, insufficient resources, weak law enforcement institutions, an ineffective judicial system, and inadequate compensation for civil service employees and public safety officials facilitate corruption." The report is then in denial, ignorance or both as to the operational reality of transnational organised crime in Belize especially the power it wields over the social order of Belize. This reality is manifested in joint organised crime enterprises between transnational organised crime, politicians and public servants. Section B. 4 of the report states that Belize lacks laws that target specifically drug related corruption. Belize does have a Prevention of

Corruption Act 2000 but no one was charged under this act in 2017. In Section B. 2. Supply Reduction the report states: "Belizean and U.S. authorities have recognised the coastal areas as rich targets for drug traffickers pushing north from South America. Belizean security organisations have limited success in limiting this criminal activity." The focus of the US is then on the coastal transition zone as a result they continue to provide equipment and training to bolster the Belizean agencies charged with policing the coastal transition zone. But according to Section B. 2 these agencies "are unable to routinely utilise assets due to insufficient resources for fuel and maintenance." But these assets provided by the US can utilise resources to transport the players and supporters of the sporting organisation connected to a minister of government. The report indicates that the US doesn't prioritise the Mexican-Belize transition zone which is today the fastest growing dual flow pipeline in Belize. The Guatemala-Belize transition zone is also not a priority. The report provides the illicit drug seizures made by the agencies of Belize for the first nine months of 2017 which illustrates the classic pattern of picking the low hanging fruit whilst leaving the prized fruit of the most valuable illicit trade untouched. Where the eradication exercise supported by the US targeting ganja plantations reportedly eradicated over 15,000 ganja plants out of a total of 17, 588 plants eradicated in 2017. Simply the politics of the war on drugs as the flow of ganja from Mexico and Guatemala continues unabated which is in fact ensuring that the hegemony over the local ganja market by the MTTOs continues which feeds the ganja wars of Southside which is now emerging in other areas of Belize. The report states that in the first nine months of 2017 59.17 kilos of cocaine and 420 grams of crack cocaine and 856.63 kilos of ganja were seized. The ganja wars of Belize are the product of the politics of the war on drugs where you target the supply side of the largest illicit drug market in Belize which distorts the market allowing members of the policing agency to then become players in this market which further distorts the supply side intensifying the violence. Whilst this is going on in the local ganja market the cocaine, heroin, meth and precursors transition zones are no go zones to the state agencies. In the report it's only in Section A. Introduction that the reality of the air pipeline into Belize is stated but not elucidated as this reality contradicts the discourse of the premier trafficking zone being the coastal areas. In fact, what is stated in the report on the air flow in no way depicts the operational reality of 2017. The primary reality of 2017 of this air bridge which has further evolved in 2018 is that the transition zone with Mexico is now a terminal point of delivery for product and a parking lot for discarded aircraft. Section A. Introduction states that the entire Belizean security sector which includes drug control is impacted negatively by the following: "corruption, insufficient investigative capacity, an ineffective judicial sector, and a lack of political will." The entire Belizean security sector in then bedevilled by the failings of a model of government the Westminster model. It's only in the final line of the report on Belize does the State Department report recognise and state the nature of the threat faced by Belize. This final line of the report in Section D. Conclusion states: "The United States will maintain its strong partnership with Belize and assist in its fight against transnational criminal organisations." The salient issue is not the partnership of the US with Belize nor the assistance the US renders but the ability of the social order of Belize to defend itself against much less to engage transnational criminal organisations operationally present in Belize. The efficacy of the assistance the US renders must then be viewed in the context of the ability of Belize to resist much less to fight and to engage with transnational organised crime. Based on the analysis of this book the US assistance rendered is then ineffective in fact futile which illustrates the inability of the Belizean social order to resist the onslaught of transnational criminal organisations.

In Volume 2 of the 2018 report the section on Belize in the Overview states: "Belize is vulnerable to money laundering due to the lack of enforcement of its laws and regulations, strong banking secrecy protections, geographic location, and weak investigative and prosecutorial capacity. The sources of money laundering are drug trafficking, tax evasion, securities fraud, and conventional structuring schemes." The Belizean state is failing to address the illicit activities generated by the financial structures and activities created by the state. The Belizean state has and is creating capacity which when coupled with the failure to investigate and to prosecute means there is no law enforcement and illegality flourishes. Much less the process of continuous legislation coupled with regulation to plug loopholes and to address new threats which results in an enabling environment to transnational organised crime a gangsta paradise! The operational landscape encompasses offshore banks, insurance companies, trust service providers, mutual fund companies and IBCs. The IBC Registry has 49,192 registered active IBCs whilst 2,165 trusts are registered at the International Trust Registry. One IBC has an online gaming license and can operate in the offshore sector a recipe for an effective laundry. There are five international banks regulated by the Central Bank and the International Financial Services Commission supervises offshore entities. Belize has two Free Trade Zones (FTZ) one at Corozal in the Mexico-Belize transition zone and the other at Benque Viejo in the Guatemala-Belize transition zone. Then there is the gaming sector of Belize which as at December 2016 comprised nine casinos or licensed gaming premises, 33 licensed gaming establishments, and three on-line gaming/internet casinos. This gaming sector is regulated by the Gaming Control Board under the Ministry of Investment, Trade and Commerce and each category/type of gaming entity is subject to a different body of different operating restrictions which must be enforced by the Gaming Control Board. The report states: "The FIU, the Police Department, and Customs and Excise Department face challenges with political interference, corruption, and human resource and capacity limitations." The politicians then willingly create the capacity that can facilitate illicit activities especially those that are of special importance to the sustainability of transnational organised crime. By their failure to ensure that an effective and evolving regulatory framework oversees the capacity created the politicians ensure that the capacity evolves into a gangsta paradise. The issue is not what motivates the politicians to not ensure that proper and necessary oversight exists rather it's their willingness to embrace all realities that flow from their failure to act pre-emptively. It's simply called pragmatism where the strategy calls for only handling realities that emerge that impact their political sustainability in a manner where the minimum action necessary to get by at a given instance is launched. In the case of money laundering and other financial crimes for Belize this is solely a geopolitical issue as it has no impact on local electoral politics. Transnational organised crime that's mindful of this rule of pragmatism and effects its strategy to minimise risk accordingly can then get away with murder having done so already. The report in its final section sums up the approach of the politicians as follows: "the government did not prosecute any money laundering cases in 2017. The low prosecution and conviction figures continue to reflect the lack of robust enforcement efforts." As geopolitical pressure is applied enough is set in train to get by governed by a process of long term implementation such as a three-year time frame. But during this process of implementation to relieve international pressure there is no qualitative change. As there is no process of investigation and prosecution resulting in conviction in a court of law in 2017. Impunity is the foundation of a gangsta paradise. From this report it's now obvious that the offshore financial sector and the gaming sector is one reason for the Russian visitors traversing Belize.

In the volume 1 of the 2017 report on Belize the discourse is unchanged from that of 2018 in fact the language is as a template where specific changes for the year are added and those of the previous year deleted. What is noteworthy in this report is how the present government of Belize is welcoming even pliant to the requests and intervention of the US in the war on drugs in Belize. But this has had no impact on the operations of transnational organised crime in Belize. For example, in 2015 the Anti-Narcotics Unit was upgraded to a U.S. - vetted unit with additional resources provided by the US and a full time DEA advisor. In 2012 the US assisted the government of Belize in the creation of the Mobile Interdiction Team comprising members of the Nationality and Immigration Department and the Belize Police Department charged with interdicting narcotics and other illicit materials entering Belize via the ports of entry. The 2017 report states that the US government is supporting the move by the MIT to establish forward operating bases in the transition zones of the north with Mexico and the west with Guatemala. The dance with the US agenda by the Belizean government is certainly not impacting negatively the operations of transnational organised crime in Belize. This is the result of the reality of the dance with transnational organised crime with politicians and public servants which successive INCSRs describe with the discourse of corruption with all its inadequacies. The US bureaucrats have then to justify the continuing US intervention in Belize that has failed to generate the change sought by the US. In the 2017 report they are seeking out good news one instance of which was the fall in serious crimes in Belize but the rise in murders in 2016 was the blemish. Sounds familiar as this is the chosen refrain of the policing agencies of the CARICOM. In April and in October 2016 with US assistance including SOUTHCOM Belize carried marijuana plantation eradication exercises but the interdiction of cocaine was dismal 17 kilos and 1 kilo of crack cocaine and as in 2017 there were no interdictions of heroin. Given the tonnage of cocaine transiting Belize the annual interdiction is in fact pathetic and speaks volumes to the game of smoke and mirrors being played by US support for Belize. This is the apparent futility of US action in Belize as in spite of all the glowing news of actions taken, rolled out and in the works the transnational organised crime groups are advancing their operations in Belize to the next evolutionary stage. The report notes that in 2016 no one was charged under the Prevention of Corruption Act which was also the reality in 2017. One strand of discourse placed in the 2016 report is embellished in the 2017 report resulting in a potent message attached. In the 2016 the strand is as follows: "Belize is bordered by countries where the drug trade is controlled by well organised and extremely violent drug trafficking organisations." Namely Mexico and Guatemala to the north and west respectively. In the 2017 report the embellished discourse is: "Belize is bordered by countries where the drug trade is controlled by well organised and violent drug trafficking organisations. A concerted effort by those organisations to establish themselves in Belize would present serious challenges to the country's law enforcement and justice institutions." The threat has now evolved for there is the possibility that Mexican and Guatemalan organised crime would now set up shop in Belize. That is how far the report is willing to go and can possibly go given the politics of the report. But the statement riven with and driven by functional denial, the bury the head up your ass syndrome, as the MTTOs are in control in Belize. The assessment of the report of the impact of these transnational organised crime groups on the social order of Belize is also understated and underrated. As is evident in Belize the impact of transnational organised crime is changing the nature of the social order.

In volume 2 of the 2017 report the discourse is the same as in the 2018 report as the means and the wherewithal to effectively regulate the sprawling financial sector created by the politicians simply don't exist especially in the case of money laundering. This failing is especially relevant given the geographical location of Belize and the operational presence of transnational organised crime in Belize especially the MTTOs. In the report it's stated that it's a common practise to move money via the two free trade zones across the borders with Mexico and Guatemala. The movement of cash generated by illicit drug sales in the US out of the US to laundries external of the US is facilitated by this cash movement in Belize. The cash pipeline through the free trade zones of Belize is then a dual flow pipeline with portions of the cash proceeds of the MTTOs entering Belize to be washed or to facilitate movement into the Caribbean island chain washing complex. The report states that Belize has a whole raft of anti money laundering laws on the statute books but the Financial Intelligence Unit mandated to enforce the regulations is a lame duck as its responsibilities far outweigh and exceeds its capacity. A lesson in the game of geopolitical brinksmanship the politicians play with international pressure seen in the statement made in the report. The statement is as follows: "Belize is making efforts to address its AML deficiencies." The fundamental operational reality is whenever Belize has solved all the listed deficiencies in its regulatory framework will these institutions be capable and willing to grapple with transnational organised crime? Will these institutions be free of joint enterprises with organised crime as is common in other ministries of government? Will these institutions be willing and capable of resisting political pressures? That then is the operational terrain of this fundamental reality. In its final section the report states: "The judiciary branch expressed concern about the sustainability of Belizean AML laws since they have not been implemented effectively. Belize investigators and prosecutors need instruction on implementation of these laws." The laws are on the books but with no impact on the operational terrain as the spear point of the rule of law is blunt and ineffective i.e. investigation and prosecution. The response to geopolitical pressure placed the laws on the statute books following this geopolitical pressure has to be applied to address efficacy and the next and the next. Who then is the beneficial owner of this strategy? The report has then to come to one conclusion as follows: "The loosely monitored offshore financial sector and the FTZs continue to be concerns."

In the Volume 1 of the report for 2016 Belize is now listed as a trafficking point for drug precursors but the report is silent on the nature and identity of the precursor/s. The report listed the interdiction of 26 kilos of heroin and 2.8 kilos of cocaine and a trace amount of methamphetamine. As per usual the emphasis of the report on drug supply reduction was on ganja i.e. how many plants destroyed and quantity of ganja seized. But in 2015 the illicit product mix in Belize has been revealed with the seizures of heroin, meth and illicit drug precursors. In subsequent reports there are no listings for interdicted heroin, meth and precursors which does not reflect the supply reality on the ground. As one of the maxims of the Game states because there is no interdiction never assume that there is no supply as you will make an ass of yourself. In the 2016 report the border with Guatemala is listed with the Belizean coastline as the premier transition zones of Belize with the coastline still in first place. This listing of the transition zone with Guatemala is not mentioned in subsequent reports but in 2015 it was common knowledge that the MTTOs were producing industrial grade meth and cocaine hydrochloride in laboratories in Guatemala. The precursor trafficked through Belize in 2015 was then for the production of industrial grade crystal meth. The report applauds the continuous fall in serious crime for fifteen years in Belize from 2000 to 2014 by 45% but this fall in serious crime is not marching in lockstep with a decline in the illicit trades as drugs and small arms trafficking. As serious crime levels decrease according to official statistics the illicit trades thrive and evolve and the murder rate escalates as does gun violence. Which means that the social order generated by the illicit trades is changing and have changed the nature and methodology of crime in Belize and the Caribbean island chain. The 2016 report illustrates that the US is cognisant of the nexus of the alternate social order with the illicit trades by the following statement: "Through CARSI the United States works with Belize to disrupt and decrease the flow of narcotics, weapons, and illicit proceeds generated by sales of illegal drugs, and to combat gangs and criminal organisations." The US is then striving to mitigate the drive to hegemony of the social order generated by the illicit trades in Belize over the formal, licit social order. Judging from the evidence to-date apparently the US investment has had little or no success in its engagement with the nexus of the illicit trades and the alternate social order. And the commonly cited reasons given in the INCSRs as "corruption" is gravely lacking in specificity and instances of actual, concrete and accurate depictions of reality on the ground. The 2016 report states in its final paragraph: "The United States encourages Belize to strengthen its public security and law enforcement institutions through more effective anti-corruption legislation, comprehensive background checks and vetting of new and existing personnel, better training, and continuing education programs." This report indicated that the

Anti-Narcotics Unit became a US vetted unit in 2014 what difference has the ANU made to the terrain of illicit drug trafficking in Belize from 2014 to 2018? This US vetted unit has failed to hinder the evolution of the illicit trade in Belize in this period. What has this vetted unit done to grapple with the marked increase in air flights that commenced in 2017 and continues in 2018? Nothing of impact to the course of the evolution of the illicit trades. On this example alone the efficacy of the discourse of corruption is gravely questioned when applied as the explanatory tool to the reality of Belize!

The Volume 2 of the 2016 report states: "There are strong indications that laundered proceeds are increasingly related to organised crime groups involved in the trafficking of illegal narcotics, psychotropic substances, and chemical precursors." Belize is then a laundry for transnational organised especially the MTTOs. The abiding question persists over the will to investigate and prosecute in spite of the raft of laws being placed on the statue books. The report states: "Despite the new laws and regulations, some international experts have said experienced staff and political will to use the new tools to actually implement an assertive program of investigation and prosecution are still necessary." This position is potently illustrated with the case of the FIU charged with the task of monitoring specific sectors with reference to money laundering and terrorist financing (AML/CFT). What has transpired with the case brought against a company operating in the offshore sector of Belize in 2014 thereby freezing its assets is illustrative of the weaknesses of the investigation and prosecution arms of the Belizean FIU. In November 2014 the Chief Justice of Belize ruled that the FIU froze the assets of the said company without fit and proper evidence provided thereby ordering the freeze ended and the assets released. This offshore company in Belize was one of six companies and six executives that the US indicted in 2014 for a USD 500 million offshore asset protection, securities fraud, and money laundering scheme utilising the Belizean offshore sector. The case brought by the FIU of Belize has collapsed. A most fitting example of the strategy of pragmatic engagement with the hegemon to the north. Hurry up and accomplish little but be very busy in the process of doing nothing.

The Misuse of Drugs (Amendment Act) 2017

Act Number 47 of 2017 was assented to on 2nd November 2017 by Governor-General Sir Colville N. Young and Gazetted on 4th November 2017. How then does this amendment that deals with the possession and smoking of ganja flow with the geopolitics of ganja with the US and the electoral politics of the UDP? The INCSRs trumpeted the US aided Belizean efforts to dismantle ganja plantations in Belize which signalled the zero tolerance approach to ganja pushed by the US. Counter to this geopolitical reality is the pragmatic where this amendment will redound to the benefit of the UDP at municipal elections in 2018 and damage control thereafter leading to general elections due in 2020. The amendment decriminalises the possession of 10 grammes and less of ganja, to put in place monetary and non-recordable penalties for possession of 10 grammes or less of ganja on school premises, in specified circumstances, to de-criminalise the smoking of ganja on private premises and to handle matters that arise from these provisions. The amended misuse of drugs act refuses to deal with the issue of licit, legal supply married to licit, legal production given the fact that the amended act creates licit, legal possession and use in private places of 10 grammes or less. The amended act refuses to relinquish the right of the state and the ruling politicians to police and punish those who choose to use 10 grammes or less of licit ganja through the power of the minister and the state to establish regulations that enable the issuance of controlled drug violation tickets. When found to have 10 grammes or less of ganja in his/her possession a regular user of licit ganja will be issued controlled drug violation tickets with a monetary fine attached. Much more significant is the refusal to allow ganja users the right to grow and produce ganja products from a stated number of ganja plants. This means that those in possession of 10 grammes or less of ganja had to enter the illicit drug market to acquire product where the act of buying is not decriminalised as is the act of growing and producing your own supply. This act has changed the dynamic of the demand side of the ganja market of Belize and this is combined with the continued assault on Belizean ganja production in the face of the demand for ganja on drug markets in Belize. The responses to these realities on the demand and supply side of the market have resulted in an intensification of the ganja wars of Belize and a ratcheting up of the smuggling of ganja into Belize from Mexico and Guatemala. The loads of ganja coming in via the coastline transition zone are increasing in response to market demand and Venezuelan grown and produced ganja is aggressively seeking Caribbean markets given the need for hard currency income to enable survival within the runaway inflationary spiral and acute foreign exchange shortage of the present Venezuelan economy. The increasing loads of ganja entering the coastline transition zone will further impact the ganja wars of Belize City. What is then obvious is that the gambit of the government in 2017 was to end the criminalisation of persons charged and convicted for possession of small amounts of ganja and allow persons so convicted and fined BD $ 1,000 and less or by another amount that the minister has power to prescribe before or after the proclamation of the amendment act to become a "specified person." The specified person is entitled to the expungement of this criminal record upon an application made in the prescribed manner. They couldn't do this without decriminalising possession and consumption of a prescribed "small amount" of ganja. This political gambit is framed then by the continuation of the war on ganja plantations in Belize, the trafficking and sale of ganja no matter the amount and possession above 10 grammes. The US targeting of ganja in Belize as the only indicator of its yield on investment in the war on drugs in Belize remains viable as the UDP government continues to do its geopolitical duty.

http://www.nationalassembly.gov.bz/wp-content/uploads/2017/04/Act-no.-47-of-2017-Misuse-of-Drugs-Amendment-1.pdf

Through three reports of the INCS Volume 1 the discourse of the State Department is constant as its driven by the following constructs. These are: the geographic location of Belize in the Central American isthmus places it in the trafficking route of illicit drugs from the south to the US, the coastline of Belize is the primary transition zone for illicit drug trafficking into Belize with illicit air flights being a distant second, the dominant strategic objective in the US engagement with Belize is to engage with and diminish illicit drug trafficking through the coastal transition zone of Belize and the institutional response of the Belizean state to the threats posed by illicit drug trafficking by transnational organised crime is inadequate to realising the strategic objective of the US. The three primary constructs frame a discourse that manufactures its own reality in order to make itself operational. The US discourse doesn't resonate nor is it organic to the reality of the Belizean drug market on the ground. The US discourse is then drinking its own Kool Aid brewed by the discourse for consumption by its target audience. The discourse is constituting itself and its audience a case of discursive incest with grave limitations and consequences. The discourse is totally unable to admit to, enumerate and state the evolutionary stages illicit drug trafficking in Belize has evolved through to-date and is continuing to evolve at present and the changing reality constituted on the ground. The US discourse is locked in stasis hence its irrelevance. As a result, the discourse of explanations addressed to the inadequacy of the institutional response of the Belizean state and the solutions proffered address a manufactured reality that has no material presence in the daily power relations of the Belizean state. Hence the solutions of the US discourse are non-solutions simply geopolitical masturbation/ jerkoff. The US discourse is part of the problem not the solution and will remain a participant in power relations that will aid and deepen the hegemony of the MTTOs over Belize rather than hinder it. Get real!

In Volume two of the three INCS reports reviewed there is an entirely different discourse and strategic approach of the US towards Belize on the issue of money laundering and terrorist financing. There is no hand holding accompanied by the flow of resources by the US to Belize that obtains for the war on drugs. The operational US discourse states that Belize has an extensive offshore sector and other financial structures that enable money laundering by dint of their organic operational modus operandi, Belize has an extensive legislative framework and institutional structure to facilitate and enable effective regulation of these sectors that can support illicit activity but the institutional structure in Belize charged with investigation and prosecution is grossly inadequate to the task of grappling with the threat horizon that exists. This institutional inertia embraces the FIU, the other regulatory institutions created by legislation and the judiciary of Belize. The US discourse insists that it's a grave human resource problem in the hiring of capable staff, continuous training of staff, staff retention, and political will. The US discourse of Volume two unlike that of Volume one does not utilise the discourse of corruption as an explanatory tool for the failure on a continuing basis to adequately regulate the financial sector of Belize. It's as if the corruption that is common to the institutions charged with the war on illicit drugs is unable to infect the financial sector and its regulation according to the US discourse. Yes, I'm wishing on a star. Two volumes of a report which indicate two different strains of geopolitical power relations driven by two distinct operational discourses which indicate a multi-personality hegemon to the north demanding compliance. This reality of geopolitical power relations is in fact a potent illustration of the power wielded by transnational organised crime in Belize through its operational presence and the organised crime enterprises in conjunction with politicians and public servants. There are limits to power even to the power of the hegemon to the north as there are limits to the power exercised by transnational organised crime, the politicians and public servants in Belize the core issue is then understanding the dynamics of the power relations of these four entities locked in a danse macabre in Belize. Explanations that are lynch pinned to a discourse of corruption can only focus on human agency measured against a yardstick of the law and sovereignty. These explanations are blind to the dynamic of power relations and human action derived thereof hence the inability to explain the reality summed up as corruption.

CHAPTER 4

The Government of Belize

Belize became independent from British colonial rule on September 21, 1981 and its independence constitution kept to the model created for the first wave of decolonisation of British colonies of the West indies in the 1960s. The government premised on the separation of powers is divided into the Legislature, the Executive and the Judiciary. The Legislature comprises the Governor-General as the Queen is the Head of State and the House of Assembly which comprises of the House of Representatives and the Senate. The Executive comprises the Cabinet headed by the Prime Minister. The Judiciary comprises the Supreme Court, the Court of Appeals, the Magistracy and the Family Court presided over by the Chief Justice with the final Court of Appeal being the Caribbean Court of Justice.

The Legislature/House of Assembly

The House of Representatives comprises 31 members/representatives elected by the constituents of 31 electoral constituencies utilising the first past the post electoral system where you can win the election for a constituency by a single vote. This electoral system manufactures a majority which has aided the appearance and operational presence in Belize of two dominant political parties: The United Democratic Party (UDP) and the Peoples' United Party (PUP) who dominate the House of Assembly. The Constitution recognises the leader of the majority party in the House of Representatives as the Prime Minister (PM) designate which means that the power relations of a political party impact the choice of political leader and the candidates chosen to contest the 31 seats of the House of Representatives long before the electorate in each of the 31 constituencies have voted in a general election. The Constitution recognises only the Prime Minister as compulsory to constituting a duly appointed government. The PM then chooses his/her Cabinet, determines its size and allocates the Ministerial portfolios as he/she sees fit. In this process the power relations of the party especially with its financiers, its party activists and with the PM impact the process. The electorate is now a remote consideration to this process. The PM can choose his/her cabinet from the House of Representatives and the Senate which can effectively emasculate the House and by extension the legislature by turning it into the lap dog of the PM. Party discipline combined with the power of the PM effectively silences the legislature leaving the executive free of effective legislative oversight.

This is illustrated by the nature of the present Cabinet of Belize. In the aftermath of the 2015 general election the UDP won 19 seats and the PUP 12 seats in the House of Representatives. The Cabinet comprises 21 members of the House of Representatives and the Senate and the Attorney General who is not a member of the House of Assembly. With two members from the Senate and 18 members from the House of Representatives of these there are 14 Ministers including the Attorney General and 7 Ministers of State appointed by the PM to aid specific Ministers. The Senate comprises of 13 members including the President the UDP has 6 members, the PUP 3 members, the business interests, the religious interests and labour and civil society each have 1 member each. The entire structure and composition of the cabinet expresses the power of the PM and the power relations that envelop the PM, the ruling party, the members of the House of Representatives and Senate. These power relations also encompass the choices for the UDP seats in the Senate, the candidates for 31 seats in the House of Representatives and the appointments to various posts etc. constituting the largesse of the state that falls to the victorious party in a general election under the Westminster model. The inclusion of 7 Ministers of State in the cabinet illustrates the power of the PM and the strategic considerations that arise but there are always limits to power borne out of resistance and this is potently indicated in this study.

The Executive

The Cabinet presently comprises 21 Ministers, Ministers of State including the Attorney General who is not a member of the National Assembly headed by the Prime Minister Dean Barrow. The 14 Ministers including the PM and the Attorney General sit at the apex of the 14 Ministries which constitute the primary platform of the Executive and embrace the agencies of the state charged with government. All agencies of the state falling under the purview of a Ministry are manned by public servants whose terms and conditions of

service and all industrial relations matters are handled by the Public Services
Commission which has 19 members including the Chairperson save and except
collective bargaining for wages and salaries where the Cabinet determines the
quantum settled on. These 19 members are appointed by the
Governor-General upon the advice of the PM and the budget of the
Commission is financed by the Ministry of Finance indicating the impact of
the ruling politicians on the Commission.

A ruling politician has a maximum five-year horizon of political action before
the next general election becomes due. The primary concern is winning
elections on a sustainable basis as under the Westminster model of government
the winner takes all and the loser is condemned to the powerless sterility of
opposition politics. The politicians must use all the resources at hand in order
to win a general election and a ruling politician must use the executive power
he/she wields in a manner they deem strategically necessary towards electoral
victory. From the outset a ruling politician has then to strive earnestly to
politicise the executive of the state especially its public service. In Belize the PM
already dominates the Legislature by having most of the government benches
in the Cabinet which means that the legislature cannot pre-empt the process
of politicisation if it wanted to. More importantly the Constitution of Belize is
devoid of agencies endowed with oversight powers to challenge the agenda of
politicising the agencies of the state.

From the outset there is then a power relation between the Minister and the
public servants of the Ministry he/she is responsible for to the PM, the
Legislature and the population of Belize. In the drive for electoral success
on a sustainable basis the ruling politicians will and must seek to supplant,
by pass and dismantle the operational procedures of the public service the
question then arises is if the Constitution of Belize recognises this political
imperative and has created an institutional structure to ensure the integrity of
the operational procedures of the Belizean state agencies? No, it has not and
do you expect the dominant politicians of the two party system to now do so?
The structural weaknesses of oversight over the public service coupled with the
unrelenting power relations with politicians to bring the public service to heel
have resulted in a public service where the policing of discipline has collapsed

as has all other industrial relations functions. When faced with the assault of transnational organised crime seeking to establish a joint criminal enterprise with public servants of strategic relevance the institutional structure of the public service cannot resist and repel, much less withstand the assault.

The agenda of politicisation favours those politicised public servants as it spreads impunity throughout the state agencies where the hierarchy of the public service collapses replaced by cells exercising varying levels of power in the structure. This breeds illicit acts which evolve into organised crime rings within the public service. When transnational organised crime enters the environment then expanse, scale and impact of the organised crime enterprise on the public service department, Ministry and the social order explode and evolve into an alternate social order where criminality is hegemonic. In this operational reality the ruling politician is brought to heel by the organised crime enterprise within the department and the wider Ministry. If the politician is not a participant in the illicit enterprise the primary concern is the political fallout and its impact personally and on the government that arises with any attempt to deal with this reality. The base instinct is to negotiate détente which works for the Minister especially as to his/her political career. If the Minister is involved in the organised crime enterprise, then all efforts are already in operation to minimise personal political risk. The state of Belize and its agencies reward those with impunity for being involved in organised crime enterprises which is a telling message to those not involved. Both public servants and ruling politicians so involved are the beneficiaries of state granted impunity.

The ruling politicians of Belize in pursuit of a sustainable basis of winning general elections must constantly work at the task of voter mobilisation and the maintenance of order which recognises the hegemony of the political elite. Voter mobilisation is then seeking means to win and maintain voter support regardless of the quality of governance and the performance of politicians especially ruling politicians. Divisions of race and ethnicity that are married to an urban/rural dichotomy and their ability to influence voters to support a specific political party is then a perceptual reality to exploit which when exploited imaginatively rewards politicians with impunity granted by strategic sections of the electorate. Impunity that breeds a specific level of political arrogance especially exhibited by ruling politicians.

The Municipal Elections of 2018

On Wednesday March 7, 2018 elections for the 9 municipalities comprising a total of 67 electoral seats contested were held with the UDP winning 41 of the 67 seats and the PUP 26 seats. But the PUP won all 11 seats in Belize City effectively taking control of the municipality of Belize City from the UDP. The PUP took Corozal Town sweeping all 7 seats and held in Orange Walk Town. The UDP won all 28 seats in the three western municipalities thereby winning the following in total: Belmopan, Benque Viejo del Carmen, Dangriga, Punta Gorda, San Ignacio/Santa Elena and San Pedro. The urban/rural divide was then in 2018 fixed and clear and the UDP in 2018 is now a rural based party. The loss of Belize City the primary urban conclave of Belize which accounts for 10 constituencies in the House of Representatives to the PUP sends a clear message to the UDP on their political sustainability as the voter base of the UDP in Belize City and by extension Belize District is key to their dominance of electoral politics in Belize in the 21st century. Hence the emphasis today on suppressing crime in Belize City and on the BPD.

http://www.reporter.bz/front-page/udp-wins-2018-municipal-election-belize-city-win-augurs-well-for-pup-in-2020/

http://amandala.com.bz/news/pup-blowout-belize-city-orange-walk-corozal/

The Belize Police Department (BPD)

Ruling politicians view the police as the main instrument to assure their rule over the social order. The police as in the colonial social order is called upon to maintain the hierarchy of the social order by dealing with threats to the social order as defined by the politicians. The high gun violence associated with the illicit trades in Belize has now politicised violent crime and the police is pressured to deal with expressions of violent crime via a criminogenic profile that fits a specific population of Belize summed up in the population of Southside, Belize City. The word used is "suppression" as in the Gang Suppression Unit of the Belize Police Department (BPD) as the politicians through the police are dealing with a reality they view as the product of an insurgency. The BPD is the agency of the state that the ruling politicians must politicise as it's the premier agency of the state apparatus central to the maintenance of the order sought by the ruling politicians of Belize. Politically desired order that ruling politicians view as being central to re-election whilst opposition politicians do everything in their power to subvert the drive of ruling politicians for.

The politicisation of the paramilitary BPD solely charged with policing the social order by the ruling politicians of Belize from independence on September 21, 1981 to the present has disrupted the command hierarchy of this paramilitary force. Politicisation endows members of the hierarchy with power which is not in keeping with their position in the command hierarchy. This breeds indiscipline in the ranks which is manifested via rogue groups and individuals throughout the entire structure. In addition, the career path of members of the BPD is impacted by politicisation and political favours for or against career advancement. The best and the brightest does not rise to the apex of the hierarchy whilst the political imperatives of the ruling politicians always weigh heavy on police action whether it's relevant to the terrain of criminality or not. Impunity pervades the organisation which coupled with the political driven policing to preserve the social order under the paramountcy of the politicians alienates the BPD from the especially the poor, the working class, the working poor and the underclass of Belize. In spaces of Belize dominated by these social groups policing is premised on "suppressing" an insurgency or a "holding action" in hostile territory. The BPD is not then organic to these spaces of the social order they are simply interlopers who invade then leave. These are spaces of the Belizean social order under the control of transnational organised crime and their local affiliates. One end result of a politicised BPD is seen in the quality of cases that are brought to the courts and criminal behaviour exhibited by members of the BPD. The repeated instances of reports from civilians on the violence waged on them by members of the BPD illustrate the nature of politicised policing in Belize and the response of the state agencies to said reports further alienate the civilian population especially amongst the profiled population of the "hotspots" from the BPD. The application of the strategy of the policisation of the BDF has now resulted in the adoption of the modus operandi of the BPD by the BDF executed with military precision. Exemplified in the case where seven members of the BDF and one member of the BPD were charged and arraigned for murder and attempted murder for beating four men at Orange Walk Town on February 22, 2018 one of whom Ariel Salazar subsequently died as a result of injuries sustained as a result of the beating. The seven soldiers were masked while delivering the beat down and were all assigned to the BDF Special Assignment Group (BSAG) at Orange Walk Town whilst the police constable was attached to the Special Patrol Unit attached to the BSAG at Orange Walk Town. What is also noteworthy in this case is the adoption of institutions, strategies and discourses by the politicians and the first division of the policing agencies of Belize and Trinidad and Tobago as if they are all reading from the same playbook whilst the game is lost.

The rising incidences of violence especially gun violence in Belize City took a new turn for 2018 with the shooting to death of reputed Southside gang leader Kendis Flowers on the weekend of March 17 to 18, 2018. The expectation of an explosion of tit for tat violence in Southside following the killing of Flowers resulted in the press conference of PM Dean Barrow on March 18, 2018 where he announced the measures taken by his government towards an intervention in Southside. The PM announced that the Ministry of Defence and the Ministry of Home Affairs will again be joined to form a single Ministry of National Security headed by John Saldivar. The BDF will be on the streets of Belize City conducting patrols and the government will utilise Section 18 of the Constitution to declare named areas of Belize City as "Emergency Areas" by requesting that the Governor-General so declare. In these areas the Police will have the powers of arrest and detention that obtain under the declaration of a state of emergency in the defined "emergency areas". A measure clearly patterned on the "Zones of Special Operations/ZOSOs" of the present JLP government of Jamaica. What is noteworthy is that the government has not addressed the increase in illicit flights into the trafficking transition zone along the border with Mexico in a similar manner nor even expressed concern with this development. In his address at the press conference on March 18, 2018 Amandala.com reports the PM as stating on the BPD as follows: "We are well aware of problems in the Police Department. We are well aware that there are some policemen, perhaps women, whose behaviour, whose interaction with the underworld, to put it mildly, leaves a lot to be desired. Again, that is part of the remit of the new expanded leadership of the Department, to try to eliminate as much as possible, that kind of a relationship which is such a keep-back in terms of the crime fighting effort." The Prime Minister again utilises the discourse of the powerlessness of the politicians when faced with the power of the public servant. The corrupt elements within the BPD are the ones to blame for the crime spiral as police corruption diminishes the capacity and capability of the BPD to ensure public safety. The elimination of corruption within the ranks of the BPD is the task of the leadership of the BPD not that of the ruling politicians. The leadership of the BPD must be blamed for the spiralling crime rate not the ruling politicians. The BPD is now the fall guy for the ruling politicians, the scape goat and when necessary the sacrificial lamb.

The incidents that occasioned the funeral of Kendis Flowers on Sunday 25 March 2018 signalled the evolution of gangland specifically the Ghost Town crew, their families and associates as child mothers at Mayflower street. The funeral of Flowers brought out the Ghost Town crew, families and associates and Flowers was given the send-off required for a ranking gangsta the 21-gun salute and the sound off. On the return of the entourage to the home of the flowers family on Mayflower street the gang suppression unit (GSU) swarmed the house and those gathered in the yard of the house in response to reports of gunfire. With the warning given in advance the gang bangers present disappeared leaving the men of the Flowers family present. A group of women openly resisted the advance of the GSU through the crowd towards the house whilst others recorded the scene as it unfurled on their cell phones. The hatred of and animosity towards the GSU was openly stated by the women especially their position that Flowers was murdered by the GSU. The confrontation between the women and the GSU led to the use of rubber bullets, pepper spray and live rounds by the GSU. The GSU entered the Flower's residence arrested one of the brothers of Kendis Flowers and left with him only to subsequently release him without charges being laid. The videos of the incident were uploaded to various social media sites. Mayflower street is the focal point of the gang turf of the Ghost Town crew of Southside where the incident potently illustrates the contested nature of the space and the policing strategy of the

GSU and the strength of the social order of gangland. Where specific women of the order are willing, able and committed to engage the GSU with only their voices and their cell phones.

A video uploaded to YouTube of the funeral procession of Flowers illustrates a mixed approach to the Crips life as in the procession there were those displaying the expected colours of the Crips with their clothes and bandannas whilst other wore white with splashes of blue and the majority wore all white outfits minus bandannas. Those in all white outfits are not necessarily non-members of the Crip set as this is a strategic trait of Caribbean gangland in the quest to be invisible. With this strategy the gang name evolves where the Crips designation is dropped but not the allegiance of the set and its linkages to the transnational Crips set affiliated to the MTTOs.

https://www.youtube.com/watch?v=iPIQLQbd45c

On April 12, 2018 an unmarked heavily tinted motor vehicle containing members of the GSU on George Street, Southside was attacked with stones thrown by persons attached to George Street. Those who gave an account of the incident to 7belizenews.com stated that the vehicle moved along George street in the drive by manner. When the vehicle suddenly stopped and reversed they began throwing stones at the vehicle whilst others ran as they were convinced that the dry by was now going down. The vehicle stopped and GSU members emerged discharging rubberised shotgun rounds at those on the street and then entered specific homes where they shot males with the rubberised shotgun rounds. Persons resident of George street remained in their homes whilst the Mobile Interdiction Team (MIT) was inserted into the area as back up. The MIT is a US funded unit specifically charged with mobile interdiction of illicit drugs and other illicit goods now utilised as a suppressing force in a contested space of gangland. Why are members of the GSU trolling George street in an unmarked heavily tinted motor vehicle in a focal point gangland turf? To what end that bolsters the rule of law was this exercise devoted to? In the case of the fracas at the Flowers residence the GSU were fully supported by the government and one expects the same with the George street incident. This is not policing governed by the rule of law in the quest to boost the rule of law this is crude, basic colonial plantation suppression under the colonial mode of power relations.

http://amandala.com.bz/news/accused-murderer-norman-slusher-28-walks/

http://www.reporter.bz/front-page/bad-cop-cases-plague-police-department/

http://amandala.com.bz/news/7-bdf-soldiers-cop-arraigned-murder-attempted-murder-charges/

http://www.reporter.bz/weekend-news/soldiers-to-be-charged-with-murder/

http://www.reporter.bz/weekend-news/prime-minister-explains-short-term-crime-strategies/

http://amandala.com.bz/news/pm-barrow-brings-bdf/

http://amandala.com.bz/news/mayflower-streetghost-town-gsu-rumble/

http://www.7newsbelize.com/sstory.php?nid=44376

From 1981 to the present the BPD was in an operational condition that rendered it unable to resist and police the onslaught of transnational organised crime in its quest to form joint organised crime enterprises with members of the BPD. The reward package offered and dispensed by TOC groups can in no way be matched and bettered by the ruling politicians. In addition, the political agenda for the BPD by the politicians of Belize made them once in power very risk averse to addressing the dysfunctionalities of the BPD much less to undertake sweeping reforms necessary in response to the impact of TOC groups on the social order of Belize. The agenda of politicians for the BPD locked them into potent power relations with the membership and command personnel of the BPD which soon questioned the political dominance of the politicians over the BPD. This potent question was heightened by the reality that the joint enterprise of members of the BPD with TOC groups in Belize produced power relations of its own which expressed the potential to question the political dominance of the politicians over sections of the BPD. The Frankenstein monster bred by the power relations between politicians and members of the BPD was now showing the ability to evolve into a Dr Jekyll and Mr Hyde when necessary as the TOC groups were now calling shots.

A most potent shock to existing power relations between members of the BPD and other state agencies came with the involvement of politicians with TOC groups. This presented an entirely new order of power relations that had to be managed as it now involved politicians, agents of the state/public servants and TOC groups in organised crime enterprises. Logistics and mediation of conflicts became major issues and as was revealed in testimonies before the Senate Committee. Solutions all centred on proxies with a public profile carrying out the orders of TOC operatives who remained in the shadows. The Fujianese transnational organised crime operation of Sister Ping moving Chinese into Belize then Mexico on their way to New York, USA and the operations of Colombian transnational traffickers in Belize were the potent early illustrations of this reality. The inclusion of politicians into organised crime enterprises impacted further the BPD and other departments of the public service where the operational presence exerted itself. Impunity flourished as those in the know were now keepers of secrets that had possible national political impact. The very political agenda that politicisation was deemed central to attaining was now in jeopardy brought about by the feeding frenzy at the state trough by ruling politicians. The feeding frenzy amongst public servants created situations where the pervasive lawlessness that ensued posed a grave threat to the very sustainability of the organised crime enterprise and that of the department of government where it was located. This also resulted in a feeding frenzy in the illicit world which posed a grave threat to the drive to realise a sustainable organised crime enterprise involving politicians and agents of the state. As the order demanded by TOC groups was now broken by hustlers seeking to feed off the feeding frenzy as they were previously excluded from or given limited access to the illicit operation in a given department of government. TOC groups can and did handle the feeding frenzy but can the politicians and the agents of the state bring the monster to heel? That is the most potent question that demands an answer in Belize today? How can you expect a politician with a five-year horizon to jettison all the measures that he/she is convinced are vitally necessary to winning power again and again? What is at fault here then is the model of government as it is an imposed import from the UK on a social order in Belize that did not and cannot organically produce the discourses vitally necessary to driving the power relations that this Westminster model thrives on. The Westminster model demands the operationalisation of the discourse of Biopolitics with its attendant mechanism and apparatus of power and power/force relations. All the social order of Belize can produce is a discourse rooted in the power relations of non-white inferiority welded to the power relations of raw colonial plantation domination. When this discursive continuum is applied to the Westminster model you can only produce a politicised state driven by colonial planation power relations where might is right and the oligarchs plunder the nation for their own benefit with the support of the politicians. It's simply a colonial planation social order with its attendant politicised state seeking

to survive in the 21st century by wearing a thin veneer of being a formal democracy. The democratic veneer was imposed by the ex-colonial massa it was not an organic product of the discursive evolution of the social order. What in fact was created by the colonial overlord in Belize was a playground for transnational organised crime groups as in the rest of the Caribbean.

The Courts and the Remand Yard

The impact of politicised policing working in conjunction with the Department of Public Prosecution (DPP), the Judiciary and the Prison on the social order of Belize is illustrated by reports on the characteristics of the prison population of Belize. In the report "Behind the Prison Gates" based on research done in 2013 at the Belize Central Prison in Hattieville by John Middleton the total prison population at the time of the study was 1, 586 persons with 591 persons on remand. Of this 591 persons 171 were on remand to the Supreme Court and 420 persons to the Magistrates' Courts. Remand prisoners in the study accounted for 37% of the total prison population of Belize and according to the report amongst this 37% were young offenders held in prison for periods of time in excess of 1 year. Amongst the adult remand population, the length of imprisonment awaiting the completion of trials is also lengthy especially those charged with murder. The majority at the time of the report were incarcerated for over two years some as high as seven years. The Court diaries are backlogged with the remand yard of the Belize Central Prison now functioning as a holding pen and a training area in the methodologies and contacts necessary for a life of crime. Politicised policing in its failure to treat with the spiral of violence in Belize continues to fill the remand prison with prisoners charged and awaiting trial whilst the judiciary fails to respond to the burden of demand placed on its judicial infrastructure especially for capital cases as murder. Then there are the limits to the granting of bail by Magistrates where the accused has to apply to a Supreme Court judge. Another measure that flows from politicised policing married to the political agenda to deal with politicised crime responses. Measures as these all neatly summed up with the political slogan of "a zero tolerance approach to crime" then fills the remand yard and clogs the court to the point where a new dynamic emerges. The remand yard of the Belize Central Prison has then evolved into the University of Crime in Belize offering various instructional modes and knowledge bases on the life of crime. Whilst fostering the evolution of prison gangs in Belize, their recruitment of foot soldiers within the prison and amongst those soon to depart for the wider social order and their inevitable assault on the power structure of the Belize Central Prison. The punitive response of the judiciary is illustrated in the report on the sentencing practice of imposing consecutive sentences on the accused found guilty such as seven consecutive 5 year sentences for robberies against tourists and 1 year for an escape. And in the case of another accused found guilty sentenced to 28 years in prison for burglaries plus 5 years each for two escapes to be served consecutively for a total of 38 years. Then there is the issue in the report of sentencing a young offender to life imprisonment minus a minimum term of imprisonment which literally means the whole of his/her life who committed the crime whilst being a minor under the laws of Belize. The judiciary is responding to the politicisation of responses to crime by being seen to be "tough on crime" as the prison university of crime churns out its graduates undeterred by the state. The Ombudsman of Belize Sixteenth Annual Report (2016) provides a breakdown of the offences of persons charged with on remand at the Belize Central Prison. Of the 474 persons on remand in 2016 251 (52.95%) were charged with murder hence not eligible for bail. The second highest category was crimes of dishonesty with 83 persons (17.51%) on remand and the third highest was violent crimes with 38 persons (8.01%) on remand. There were 20 persons (4.21%) on remand for drug offences and 1 (0.21%) for immigration offences. The bread and butter of the TOC groups in Belize are then not the primary concern of policing in Belize as politicised policing remains actively concerned with murders. Of the 474 persons on remand 263 persons (55.48%) have been in remand for 1 year and less whilst 211 (44.51%) persons have been incarcerated for more than 1 year. Of this 211 persons 201 (95.26%) have been incarcerated in remand for more than 1 year and up to 7 years. These statistics then confirm the acute constipation that characterises the operations of the Belizean judiciary in 2016.

A news report on reporter.bz in January 2016 reported that the Chief Justice of Belize Kenneth Benjamin has stated that the situation of prisoners on remand at the Belize Central Prison was unacceptable. Chief Justice Benjamin indicated that as at December 31, 2015 there were 403 persons on remand with 186 persons awaiting trial in the Supreme Court predominantly for murder. Twenty-seven persons are in remand for over 5 years. The Chief Justice stated that the trial process is characterised by adjournments, reluctant and recalcitrant witnesses and numerous voir dire hearings. In response to these operational realities the amendments to the Criminal Procedure Rules came into effect in January 2016.

In a news report on Amandala.com in January 2015 it was reported that the Chief Justice had stated that 2015 was to be a year of reform for the judiciary. The reforms were listed as follows: new criminal procedure rules to come into effect in 2015, new police guidelines on the interviewing and treatment of persons in detention and rules to enable magistrates and judges to disclose the sentences that will be handed down following an early guilty plea by the accused. On the impact of the new criminal procedure rules the Chief Justice stated: "No person shall await trial in the Supreme Court for more than two years with shorter time limits being applied to persons in custody on remand and to Magistrates Courts matters tried summarily." The new police guidelines to be introduced by the Commissioner of Police are formulated to address allegations of brutality and confessions obtained by force from the accused by the police. And the Cabinet is considering a draft bill to enable witnesses to give anonymous testimony. It must be noted that the new criminal procedure rules came into effect in January 2016. In a report on Amandala.com in January 2015 the Chief Justice is reported as stating that in the criminal division of the

Supreme Court the disposal rate of cases continues to be unsatisfactory largely due to the length of trials. On the conviction rate for the criminal division in 2013 the Chief Justice reported that it was 39% but the conviction rate for murder in 2013 was 8%. Given the evolution of the murder rate of Belize this conviction rate illustrates the abysmal performance of politicised policing in Belize.

A news report on Amandala.com in September 2017 indicated that the Chief Justice had failed to deliver 28 judgments to-date in cases heard before him. As a result, litigants have been waiting some 2 to 5 years for the Chief Justice to deliver the outstanding judgments. The Chief Justice has undertaken to deliver all outstanding judgments by December 2017. At a meeting of its membership held on September 15, 2017 the Bar Association of Belize passed a resolution which states: "the Chief Justice's failure to discharge his constitutional duty to afford litigants a fair hearing within a reasonable time constitutes misbehaviour in office." "the Bar Association of Belize has lost confidence in the Hon. Chief Justice's ability to perform and discharge the functions of his Office." The Bar Association stated that with the failure to deliver the outstanding judgments by December 2017 they expect the Chief Justice to resign his post and failure to do so will result in action for him to be removed by the Judicial and Legal Services Commission. A news report on Amandala.com in the month of December 2017 reported that the number of cases with outstanding judgments from the Chief Justice was now 32 and he was unable to clear this backlog by the end of December 2017. What is interesting in this development is the action proposed by PM Dean Barrow to end the backlog which was to hire two judges who did not officiate at the 32 cases to write up the judgments for them which resulted in the PM stating in the House of Representatives that the Chief Justice was averse to this proposal and the Attorney General confirmed that no additional judges will be hired. It was the Attorney General who then publicly stated that the Chief Justice will strive to deliver judgments for 22 outstanding cases and made other statements which indicated the existing relationship between the Chief Justice and the Attorney General. The Attorney General states: "But a couple weeks ago, he told me that he had full intention of completing at least twenty-two of them. Yesterday he told me that he did complete twenty-two of the judgments, and so he is still ten short, but out of the thirty-two we can say that he has concluded a significant number of those judgments." The Attorney General is now handling the spin on this political issue for the Chief Justice. An issue that is now politicised. The Attorney general continues: "So I am sure the Bar Association will take a position on it, but I think that the Chief Justice has now fully appreciated, I mean he always did appreciate the impact of not delivering the judgments, but he has now fully appreciated the extreme seriousness of it. So from now on we hope that he would do more to ensure that that type of backlog does not build up anymore, and he has every confidence of that going forward." The Attorney General continues: "Come next year he will have to find the time in addition to the duties that he has on a day to day basis. He just has to find the time to produce them, and it's not that he doesn't want to produce them. He wants to produce them, so let's see what happens in the New Year."

The spin discourse of the Attorney General is presenting a contrite and penitent Chief Justice cognisant of his sin against the judiciary and the State of Belize. The Chief Justice is not presenting any spin discourse to the public on his behalf the politicians have now filled the breach created as a result of the political fallout from the failure of the Chief Justice to deliver 32 outstanding judgments. The Attorney General is then the designated politician to be the mouth piece of the Chief Justice and the spin doctor on the issue of 32 delayed judgments in the public domain. This spin discourse is to the benefit of the politicians as the Attorney General a politician appointed by the Prime Minister is chastising and setting performance standards for the Chief Justice in public. The spin discourse expresses the power of the politicians over the judicial process not that of the Chief Justice so much for the separation of powers. The response of the Chief Justice to this power relation was revealed in a news report dated December 28, 2017 on Kaiteurnewsonline.com which reported that Chief Justice Kenneth Benjamin of Belize was chosen to fill the post of Chancellor of the Judiciary of Guyana. Whilst the political blowback from the delay in delivering judgments for thirty-two outstanding cases rippled through the public domain the Chief Justice sought, in one instance that became public, in Guyana to depart the post as head of the Judiciary of Belize. Whatever the outcome of the political game to fill the post of Chancellor in Guyana with the Chief Justice of Belize, which remains unresolved at the time of writing, he has issued the signal that he is seeking the means to exit the post of Chief Justice of Belize.

http://www.deathpenaltyproject.org/wp-content/uploads/2014/11/14.11.18-DPP-Belize-Report-PRINT-version.pdf

http://ombudsman.gov.bz/wp-content/uploads/2017/06/The-16th-Annual-Report-of-the-Ombudsman2.pdf

http://www.reporter.bz/general/supreme-court-addresses-plight-of-prisoners-on-remand/

http://amandala.com.bz/news/criminal-justice-system-reform-2015-chief-justice-benjamin/

http://amandala.com.bz/news/bar-associations-ultimatum-chief-justice-benjamin-deliver-resign-removed/

http://amandala.com.bz/news/chief-justice-kenneth-benjamin-conclude-backlog-cases-legal-year/

https://www.kaieteurnewsonline.com/2017/12/28/prospective-chancellor-has-questionable-record/

A news report on Amandala.com dated August 19, 2017 reported on the data by the Kolbe Foundation on the ethnicity of prison and remand inmates at the Belize Central Prison for January to June 2017. A total of 1,297 inmates made up the prison population for the period with the Creole ethnicity accounting for 650 inmates (50.11%) with the Hispanic ethnicity second with 326 inmates (25.13%). The crime profile of the Creole offender was vastly different from that of the Hispanic offender. There were 184 Creoles incarcerated as a result of a charge for murder or 28.30 % of Creoles incarcerated compared to 47 Hispanics or 14.41% of Hispanics incarcerated. There were 180 Creoles incarcerated for crimes of dishonesty (27.69%) compared to 59 Hispanics (18.09%). There were 73 Creoles incarcerated for firearms offences (11.23%) compared to 25 for Hispanics (7.36%). There were 58 Creoles incarcerated for violent crimes (8.92%) compared to 21 Hispanics (6.44%). The crime hierarchy of incarcerated Hispanics was as follows: 1st immigration offences (91); 2nd crimes of dishonesty; 3rd murder, 4th firearm offence, 5th drug trafficking and 6th violent crime. For Creoles it was as follows: 1st murder, 2nd crimes of dishonesty, 3rd firearms offences, 4th violent crimes, 5th drug trafficking and 6th sexual crimes, manslaughter and attempted murder. The 2010 population and Housing Census of Belize lists the ethnic composition of Belize by percentage of the three largest groups as follows: Mestizo/Spanish/Latino 52.9%, Creole 25.9%, Maya 11.3%. Why then is the Creole group way overrepresented in the prison population compared to its percentage of national population? In the 2010 census 56.5% of the population of the Belize District polled responded that they were Creole whilst 22.0% of those polled in the Stann Creek District and 18.5% in the Cayo district did so reply. Whereas for the Mestizo/Spanish/Latino 34.5% of respondents in the Belize District said they were Mestizo/Spanish/Latino with 79.7 % in the Orange Walk District, 79.3% in the Corozal District, 67.5% in the Cayo district and 33.9% in the Stann Creek District. Table HC6.2 of the 2010 Population and Housing Census reports that of the 112 murders/manslaughter recorded in Belize in 2010, 59 were in the Belize District and 30 in the Cayo district. For 2010 the Belize District and the Cayo District were the murder centres of Belize. This also holds true for robbery, burglary and wounding/assault/harm. Belize District, in which Belize City is located, is the murder capital of Belize and the focal point of violent crime in Belize followed by the Cayo district. Belmopan the capital of Belize and San Ignacio, the second and third largest cities of Belize, are located in the Cayo District which is part of the western transition zone with Guatemala. There is then a disparity between the crime levels of the urban centres and the rural areas of Belize where in the urban areas the power relations of the illicit trades of the transition zones that drive violence are overwhelmingly expressed.

http://amandala.com.bz/news/male-inmates-belize-central-prison-creole-female-inmates-hispanic/

http://sib.org.bz/wp-content/uploads/2017/05/Census_Report_2010.pdf

CHAPTER 5
The Discourse of Corruption in the Context of Belize

The cry of corruption is in fact a political act in Belize. This political act can have different aims such as replacing the present UDP with a political alternative of your choice. Or it can be the instrument of those who have a vision of a Belize that is qualitatively different from what they say it is at present but insist that they are not pursuing an agenda of a mainstream political party. In all possible cases and scenarios these constitute political acts given the operational nature of the Westminster model in Belize particularly the politicisation of the state and the social order. The fundamental and pressing questions are then: what constitutes this discourse of corruption therefore necessitating a deconstruction of the discourse and more importantly what is its operational traction in the Belizean social order? Does this discourse of corruption and its mechanism and apparatus of power enable it to grapple with joint organised crime enterprises comprising TOC groups, ruling politicians and public servants located within state institutions charged with daily government?

This discourse of corruption is a North Atlantic creation uncritically adopted and applied in Belize as in other post-colonial/neo-colonial social orders where the Westminster model was imposed by the British colonial overlord. The discourse of corruption is organically matched to the Westminster model as they are both creations of the political apparatus of the discourse of Biopolitics. They both share common discursive DNA and are therefore compatible with each other but in the operational terrain of Belize this common DNA bond has been severed. For with initial contact with the colonial social order on application and with operational evolution of the Westminster model over time the discursive DNA has mutated where the discourse of the racist colonial planation social order is now hegemonic as the discourse of Biopolitics has now become a subservient, peripheral and silenced discourse. This is exhibited potently by the prevailing position of the LGBT community in Belize and the rest of the former British colonies of the Caribbean in 2018. When you use the discourse of corruption as an analytic tool of the Belizean social order you are then utilising a powerless discourse to analyse a contrary, hegemonic discourse which means you are viewing reality via perceptive tools that are irrelevant to that reality as it does not and cannot constitute that reality. Worse yet it cannot grapple with and deconstruct the complex realities of human perception and action constituted by the hegemonic discourse which results in solutions proffered that are non-solutions. For they are solutions generic to the discourse of corruption not of the hegemonic discourse. This is why the use of the discourse of corruption is simply now political acts driven by the hope of political mobilisation in other words a political slogan that has been captured by the political actors of the political order of Belize. For the discourse of corruption cannot see the reality in its complex entirety and formulate solutions to the problems it envisages much less for the organic problems generated by the mechanism and apparatus of power of the hegemonic discourse.

The World Bank defines corruption as follows: "A corrupt practise is the offering, giving, receiving or soliciting, directly or indirectly, anything of value to influence improperly the actions of another party." This definition is gravely challenged to describe the operational nature of an organised crime enterprise involving TOC groups, politicians and public servants where there is strategy, order and measures constantly formulated and applied to attain sustainability the most potent of which is impunity in all its forms particularly in a politicised social order political impunity. In addition, there is no guarantee that with a change of political party in power the organised crime enterprises will simply dry up and disappear as TOC groups and public servants are poised and exercise the power to ensure sustainability in the face of the potential game of musical chairs that is electoral politics. The solutions proffered by the discourse of corruption simply cannot address this reality of an organised crime enterprise. Solutions as procurement legislation, an integrity commission and other legislation cannot address the operational reality of a joint organised crime enterprise with TOC groups, politicians and public servants. For they are formulated for a reality constituted by a discourse that is not hegemonic in Belize. To address the Belizean reality, you must start at the point of dealing with the Frankenstein monster that is the Westminster model. But which politicians in their quest for power will willingly agree to change the constitution to their detriment by reducing the power they wield over the social order and by extension challenging their social power? Will the politicians agree to constitutional change that emancipates the legislature from the hegemony of the Prime Minister? Will they agree that the basis for this act of emancipation is to change the electoral system the British colonial overlord attached to the Westminster model? For what is fundamentally necessary is the de-politicisation of vast swaths of the social order and to do this you need much more political engagement and horse trading. Will the politicians ensure a Public Services Commission having the resources, the staffing, the members of the Commission and an operational mode necessary to the proper functioning of the public service of Belize? Will the politicians willingly reduce the level of politicisation of the public service especially the Belize Police Department? The questions are many but the answer is simple: No! The hegemonic discourse is ensuring the sustainability of its mechanism and apparatus of power and in doing so the terrain of organised crime especially transnational organised crime is especially favoured by this survival mechanism. The apparatus of power of the hegemonic discourse of power in Belize initially favoured the oligarchs of Belize and the ruling politicians where the special relationship that developed under colonial domination expanded and evolved with independence. TOC groups penetrated this oligarchy and became part of it this opened the pathway for the dance with ruling politicians and public servants. This evolving presence and growing power over the Belizean social order is the product of the hegemonic discourse of the Belizean social order not the generic political slogan "corruption." The gift of the Westminster model to Belize is the joint organised crime enterprises located within organs of the state not "corruption" as it cannot describe the expanse, nature and impact of this reality.

The World Bank attempts to strengthen the expanse of its discourse of corruption by including within the discourse the following horizons: fraud, collusion, coercion and obstruction but refuses to recognise and state that with the inclusion of these horizons they have entered the realm of organised crime. Much more importantly the World Bank refuses to admit that regardless of the status and position of those in government and the public service involved in an organised crime enterprise at some point in the operational existence of this enterprise effecting harm to others becomes necessary for a variety of reasons. Primarily emanating from the ever pressing need to mitigate threats to the organised crime enterprise and/or from the personal impunity enjoyed by individuals within the ambit of the organised crime enterprise where recklessness and hubris flow from this impunity. The slide to violence is the most pervasive threat to the sustainability of the joint organised crime enterprise. A joint organised crime enterprise comprising TOC groups, ruling politicians and public servants as is the case in Belize exhibit a particularly volatile tendency as there are pressures applied from the world of organised crime, politics and the law. To ensure sustainability national politics and the law have then to be muted whilst TOC groups have to constantly ensure the sustainability of the hegemonic order which requires purges as the need arises. Violence is then a given in this social order as exhibited in Belize. TOC groups act to ensure the sustainability of the enterprise by co-opting sections of the oligarchy of Belize, by cultivating links with all political entities and most importantly by having as their affiliates strategic members of the BDF and the BPD. This is especially the strategy of the MTTOs. The core question then deals with the ability of the Belizean state to resist and repel this assault from TOC groups? In the search for answers the discourse of corruption is stunningly silent given the widespread uncritical mouthing of this discourse in the political and academic discourses of the English speaking Caribbean. Maybe this is the reason for its wide acceptance!

The World bank defines collusion as: "A collusive practice is an arrangement between two or more parties designed to attain an improper purpose, including influencing improperly the actions of another party." And it defines coercion as follows: "A coercive practice is impairing or harming, or threatening to impair or harm, directly or indirectly, any party or property of the party to influence improperly the actions of a party." Clearly this discourse of the World Bank cannot see the existence of organised crime enterprises within the realm of corruption. This discourse views these actors as "white collar criminals" not organised crime operatives. Where is the collusion in an organised crime enterprise involving TOC groups, politicians and public servants? Where is the collusion in an organised crime enterprise involving politicians, public servants and others who then enter into a joint venture criminal enterprise with TOC groups? This construct of collusion as is the case with the construct of corruption views the state official as being the product of the discourse of law and sovereignty who can never be the much maligned and differentiated from the mass of descent and respectable society: the common criminal. This product of law and sovereignty can only collude or be coerced into corruption as defined by the World Bank. The reality of an organised crime enterprise comprising TOC groups, politicians, public servants and others and worse yet the reality of an organised crime enterprise actively seeking transnational organised crime partners formed by politicians, public servants and others towards realising and satisfying the quest/desire for sustainable power and the maximisation of profit is totally unfathomable by this World Bank discourse. In these realities that emerge from the social order of Belize the distinction between collusion and coercion all hitched to the master operative concept of corruption has no traction on the ground. They are blind to the reality hence of very limited value as heuristic tools. They simply constitute jerk off analysis and solutions for another reality not that of Belize. To apply said solutions is but another travesty as the Westminster model applied is!

The World Bank discourse of corruption where fraud is differentiated from corruption defines fraud as follows: "A fraudulent practice is any act or omission, including a misrepresentation, that knowingly or recklessly misleads or attempts to mislead, a party to obtain a financial or other benefit or to avoid an obligation." But fraud and corruption are the outcomes of the daily operation of an organised crime enterprise rooted in state agencies of Belize this reality is a given and it's a group based activity. The issue then is the impact of deception and fraud upon the power relations of these organised crime enterprises and the manner in which these conflicts are resolved. For in an organised crime enterprise violence to resolve conflict is a given, understood and must be managed given the threat it poses to the sustainability of the organised crime enterprise. When its situated in a state structure of government then the threat posed surpasses that posited by the discourse of corruption. What is vitally necessary is a discourse of state based organised crime and the means to dismantle it in Belize. As with fraud the World Bank conceptualises obstruction as being a condition differentiated from corruption and defines it as: "An obstructive practice is deliberately destroying, falsifying, altering or concealing of evidence material to the investigation or making false statements to investigators in order to materially impede a World Bank Group investigation." This concept off the World Bank is triggered by an investigation therefore obstruction is a defensive measure by the entity under investigation. In the daily operational realm of organised crime dispersing the trail of evidence is an imperative given the certain expectation of incursions from agencies of the state. In Belize the organised crime enterprises are located in state agencies of government and are manned by public servants and politicians which embellishes these organised crime enterprises with the impunity afforded by the political and public service structures of Belize. Files are disappeared, actions never recorded in files or selectively recorded when a file is opened and when there is an investigation when the need arises files disappear or are censored. There is then a strategy made up of counter measures in place to pre-empt dismantling and punishment of the operatives of the organised crime enterprise. The strategy calls for zero instances for the need for the use of obstruction for its use indicates the failure to ensure the security of the criminal enterprise through the application of the necessary countermeasures. This is the daily operational maxim of transnational, globalised organised crime groups and the MTTOs in Belize exercising hegemony are masters of it. What is illustrative in Belize is the fingering of politicians and public servants in the public domain whilst the TOC groups remain anonymous. This is as a result of the application of the strategy of countermeasures and the silence purchased with the power of the MTTOs over the Belizean social order. The World Bank concept of obstruction as with the others in its discourse of corruption sees only a reality it conjures up a reality that has no traction on the ground and terrain of Belize hence its part of the problem not the solution.

http://www.worldbank.org/en/about/unit/integrity-vice-presidency/what-is-fraud-and-corruption

Transparency International adopts a different discourse from that utilised by the World Bank by locating theirs in government, the state and politics. Transparency International defines corruption as follows: "Generally speaking as 'the abuse of entrusted power for private gain.' Corruption can be classified as grand, petty and political depending on the amounts of money lost and the sector where it occurs." Corruption for Transparency International applies exclusively to the operation of a state by those so charged with the task of administering the state. Ranging from the politicians to the public servants and all those so appointed to execute functions necessary to the functioning of the state and the public domain. It is only through the definitions of grand, petty and political corruption by Transparency International that some clarity is afforded the reader. Grand corruption is defined as: "Grand corruption consists of acts committed at a high level of government that distort policies or the central functioning of the state, enabling leaders to benefit at the expense of the public good." "Petty corruption refers to everyday abuse of entrusted power by low-and mid-level public officials in their interactions with ordinary citizens, who often are trying to access basic goods or services in places like hospitals, schools, police departments and other agencies." "Political corruption is a manipulation of policies, institutions and rules of procedure in the allocation of resources and financing by political decision makers, who abuse their position to sustain their power, status and wealth." This discourse of corruption is hinged on acts of public officials that are undertaken for the benefit of the personal interest of the public official but are all such acts illegal under the law of the land where they are committed? It must be law to determine what is the public good and a corrupt act "at the expense of the public good" Transparency International has then to define all that precedes with the proviso "enabling leaders to benefit at the expense of the public good." But what does it mean and entail especially since there is a burden of proof that must be borne towards prosecution under law. Much more importantly is the questionable rigour of the Transparency International discourse when applied to the transnational organised crime terrain of the Belizean state agencies. For the discourse reeks of an agenda of pushing a discourse in the quest for traction and hegemony rather than as the cornerstone of intervention. This is clearly illustrated in the definition of political corruption where the discourse is either naïve on the nature of politics and its organic relationship with power or the discourse is seeking to intervene in social orders around the world in a political manner towards discursive hegemony which begets power for its adherents. All politicians must be driven by the quest for the holy grail of sustainable re-election or a hold on power of whatever nature. How then do you differentiate between political corruption and the quest for power which is compulsory in the realm of politics of whatever type? When does the quest for power evolve into political corruption? In the discourse of corruption of Transparency International framed by loose, undefined language the designation is in the eye of the beholder. This discourse is an essentially political act when executed in the neo-colonial world an act exercising discursive imperialism. The Transparency International discourse of corruption is of little analytical value for stripping bare the organised crime terrain of Belize. Its utility value is to assail the government via the discourse calling for "civil society" action to ensure "transparency" in the daily operations of government. Buzz words and catch phrases unleashed without questioning the relevance and accuracy of them in the context of the Belizean social order. Much less to question the relevance and accuracy of these buzz words to the reality of the North Atlantic states say for example Italy. This discourse is devoid of operational devices which enable and drive intervention towards reducing the instances of corruption. In addition, it focuses on politicians failing to indicate its knowledge of the power relations of states and how they impact the actions of politicians. It presents the illusion of hegemonic power wielded by politicians but daily reality in the power relations of government reveal the limits to the power of politicians and those individuals and groups that move to limit the power of politicians and exert theirs. Instance of these power relations are the power games between politicians, their financiers, the oligarchs, the activists of the ruling political party and the public servants /agents of the state. This is a landscape of shades of grey where power constantly rubs up against law. The discourse of Transparency International attempts to represent this complex reality via a discourse of distilled reality which is a discourse with political intent. Which is evident in their press release dated 21 February 2018 which states that Latin America and the Caribbean have made progress in the fight against corruption which for them is indicated by: the existence of laws and mechanisms to curb corruption, the advance of legal investigations into corrupt practices and citizen anti-corruption movements are growing across the continent. But according to Transparency International countries of the region continue to score poorly on the Corruption Perception Index 2017 produced by the organisation and they proffer their rationale in keeping with their discourse. This conundrum is explained by an alternate discourse by insisting that either the instrument that drives the Corruption Perception Index 2017 is flawed or in spite of all the profound change for the better persons polled in the continent are not perceiving a change for the better in their daily living reality. And this is so because of all the profound change Transparency International shouts about they are cosmetic as the power relations that drive the illicit enterprises geared to plunder the state are all unaffected. The profound change shouted about are simply countermeasures launched to ensure the sustainability of criminal enterprises. The sophist rationale of the discourse of corruption of Transparency International is potently illustrated by this statement in the said press release: "To truly improve anti-corruption efforts in Latin America and the Caribbean governments must foster political will and demonstrate a long-term commitment to anti-corruption reforms." The very solution proffered by Transparency International has already been falsified by their own perceptions index and their discourse of corruption. The respondents polled for the perception index are insisting that Satan cannot forgive sin, the discourse of corruption of Transparency International insists that all sin emanates from Satan/politicians but the press release is now calling on Satan/politicians to forgive sin thereby ending the propensity to sin. A convoluted, bi-polar even schizoid discourse of power hence of very little analytical value to understanding the terrain of transnational organised crime in Belize.

https://www.transparency.org/what-is-corruption

https://www.transparency.org/news/feature/
perceptions_remain_unchanged_despite_progress_in_the_americas

By Way of Pause

By dint of its geographic position Belize became on operational transition zone for transnational organised crime starting with the Colombian transnational traffickers to today where the Mexican Transnational Trafficking Organisations (MTTOs) dominate the illicit trades of Belize. Belize achieved its independence in 1981 at the cusp of the rise of Mexico and Mexican traffickers as the premier trafficking zone to the drug markets of the USA. This is the basis of the evolution of the late 20th and early 21st centuries where the MTTOs exercised hegemony over the illicit trades of the Western Hemisphere. From its birth the Belizean state rooted in the Westminster model of the Caribbean island chain was faced with the premier and plausible threat to its existence and evolution posed by transnational organised crime. The British colonial state failed miserably to resist and repel the onslaught of the transnational trafficking organisations on it from the decade of the 1960s to 1981. By independence in 1981 wide swaths of the Belizean social order and the colonial state were involved in organised crime ventures with the transnational trafficking organisations. Politicians, public servants, colonial officials and Belizean oligarchs, their families and clans were ensuring that Belize evolved into the transition zone the transnational traffickers were desirous off and willing to make you rich in order to attain it. Independence in 1981 simply meant that the Westminster model of government was placed as a veil over a social order with no organic link to it and with the mechanism and apparatus of power penetrated by, suborned by and under the assault of transnational organised crime. The Westminster model rather than resisting and repulsing the assault could have mustered only one response the duality of denial with complicity. The Westminster model of government then ensured the throttling of the Belizean state by transnational organised crime in the decade of the 1980s and 1990s.

It must be understood that the MTTOs exercise a strategic agenda very much different from that of the various Colombian transnational trafficking organisations that impacted the Belizean state and social order previously. This strategic agenda is already being written on the ground via a new order and its impact on the Belizean state and social order is evident. The evolution of Belizean gangland, the introduction of new trafficking methodologies in the Belizean transition zones all point to a resilient momentum which intends to capture agencies of the state through forming organised crime ventures with public servants/agents of the state. In this the MTTOs deliberately target members of the security apparatus of the state who possess the skill set they require and adopt them as affiliates in the illicit trafficking pipelines. You are not paid bribes you become traffickers in your own right. The MTTOs and their partners and affiliates from the ranks of transnational organised crime are then on an ongoing basis formulating and unleashing countermeasures to mitigate the threats to the organised crime enterprises they are involved with in Belize. One potent countermeasure is to unleash a tsunami of trafficking on Belize that literally inundates and brings to its knees the Belizean state. The drug flights to the transition zone with Mexico are now exhibiting the mixture of flights where the aircraft are not destroyed with those where the aircraft is destroyed but there is no abandoned intact aircraft on the ground. This suggests transition flights carrying product from Belize to a trafficking point external of Belize. The tsunami is then growing in strength. The particular lesson is that transnational organised crime constantly evolves in order to ever pursue the goal of sustainability and the maximisation of profits. And it must never be forgotten that the quantum of resources transnational organised crime involved in Belize commands dwarfs that by the state of Belize. The discourse of law and sovereignty is then the veil that renders the Belizean state open for business to transnational organised crime.

http://www.reporter.bz/crime/how-many-drug-planes-were-there/

The diversity of organised crime ventures within agencies of the Belizean state illustrate the depth and expanse of the penetration of the state by transnational and local organised crime. Organised crime is then organic to the functioning of agencies of the Belizean state and these deep rooted illicit enterprises are not being dismantled by those charged with protecting the state. Politicians come and go, public servants come and go and transnational and local organised crime operatives come and go but organised crime relentlessly indicates its uncanny ability to replicate itself sustainably across time. This is the primary potent lesson of transnational Italian organised crime especially the Calabrian Ndrangheta. Organised crime in Belize is today deep rooted, self-perpetuating and sustainable. And the responses to the scandals in the public domain with reference to corrective measures taken in response are all heavily infected with political action towards damage control devoid of the intent to dismantle the illicit enterprise. This is simply the veil of the Westminster model in action for its incapable of the required effective action. The necessary structures and measures to effect effective action simply does not exist in the constitution of Belize. The Westminster model is then powerless in the face of the hegemony of the neo-colonial planation social order and both combatants are unable to resist and repel the assaults of transnational organised crime. Belize is much more than a victim of geography for the great experiment of independence has failed as in the rest of the English speaking Caribbean.

The abiding issue that arises from this study deals with the organic ability of the Belizean state in 2018 to adequately respond, repel and regenerate in the face of the infection of organised crime of its body politic and social order. The Italian model teaches that the most momentous product Italian history has given to the world is Italian transnational organised crime and today there is an Italian state that has formed an organic relationship with transnational organised crime forming a hybrid state form. The Belizean experience must be viewed in this context where a hybrid state encompassing joint enterprises of transnational organised crime with politicians and public servants is already evolving with a range of probable and possible state forms in the works. Simply a work in progress. Pax Mexicana!

Map.

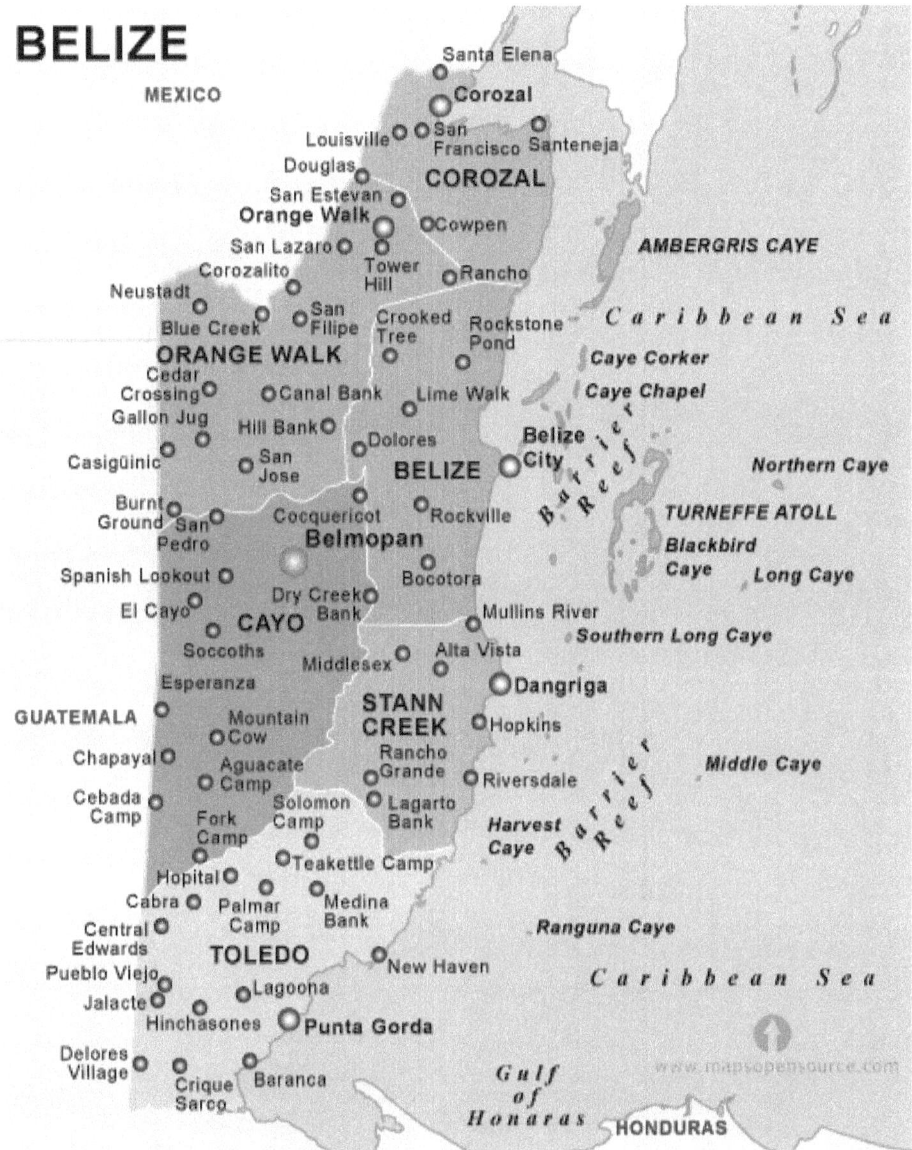

Map showing the districts of Belize and key places.

(Maps courtesy: www.mapsopensource.com[1])

---

1. http://www.mapsopensource.com

Author's Biography

Daurius Figueira is a social researcher and analyst based in the twin island Republic of Trinidad & Tobago, West Indies. His primary areas of research and publication are: the illicit drug trade, the illicit small arms trade and human smuggling in the Caribbean, Islamic Extremism with an emphasis on Salafi Jihadi discourse, the Politics of Race and Ethnicity with an emphasis on the discourse of white supremacy and non-white inferiority and the Geopolitics of Liquefied Natural Gas (LNG).

Daurius has previously published fourteen books as follows: "Cocaine and the Economy of Crime in Trinidad and Tobago" 1997, "A Spy in the Houses of Hate" 2000, "Jihad in Trinidad and Tobago July 27th 1990" 2002, "Simbhoonath Capildeo: Lion of the Legislative Council Father of Hindu Nationalism in Trinidad and Tobago" 2003, "Exiting a Racist Worldview" 2004, "The Al Qaeda Discourse of the Greater Kufr" 2004, "Cocaine and Heroin Trafficking in the Caribbean: The Case of Trinidad and Tobago, Jamaica and Guyana" 2004, "Cocaine and Heroin Trafficking in the Caribbean: Vol. 2" 2006, "Tubal Uriah Butler of Trinidad and Tobago Kwame Nkrumah of Ghana: The Road to Independence" 2007, "The East Indian Problem in Trinidad and Tobago 1953-1962 Terror and Race War in Guyana 1961-1964" 2009, "The Politics of Racist Hegemony in Trinidad and Tobago" 2010, "Salafi Jihadi Discourse of Sunni Islam in the 21st Century the Discourse of Abu Muhammad al-Maqdisi and Anwar al Awlaki" 2011, "Cocaine Trafficking in the Caribbean and West Africa in the Era of the Mexican Cartels" 2012, "The Geo-Politics of LNG in Trinidad and Tobago and Venezuela in the 21st Century" 2014.

You can visit his website at: https://www.daurius.com

Twitter: @dauriusfigueira

Facebook: https://www.facebook.com/dauriusf/

Also by Daurius Figueira

Discourse of Slavery
Massa's White Supremacist Discourse of West Indian Negro Slavery
Deconstructed Volume 1
Massa's White Supremacist Discourse of West Indian Negro Slavery
Deconstructed Volume 2

Frantz Fanon for the 21st Century
Frantz Fanon for the 21st Century Volume 1 Frantz Fanon's Discourse of
Racism and Culture, the Negro and the Arab Deconstructed
Frantz Fanon for the 21st Century Volume 2 Frantz Fanon's Discourse of
Decolonisation and Violence, the Nature of Power and Power Relations of
Neo-colonial African States,
Frantz Fanon for the 21st Century Volume 3 The Algerian Revolution, Islamic
Discourse, the Colonizer and the Discourse of White Supremacy

Standalone
Belize: Human Smuggling, Transnational Organised Crime, Politicians And
Public Servants
Biopower, Racism, State Racism and The Modern/Post Modern North
Atlantic State: Michel Foucault's Genealogy of the Historico-Political
Discourse of Race War Deconstructed

Derek Walcott's Poetry Deconstructed, Its Political and Sociological Discourse Revealed

Transnational Organized Crime and Drug Trafficking in the Second Decade of the 21st Century in the Dominican Republic, Suriname, Venezuela, French Guiana, Martinique and Guadeloupe

The Islamic State and the Muslims of Trinidad and Tobago in the 21st Century

A Deconstruction of Michel Foucault's 1979 Discourse of Neo-Liberalism for the 21st Century

A Deconstruction of Qu'ranic Discourse for the 21st Century

Watch for more at https://www.daurius.com.

About the Author

Daurius Figueira is a researcher, analyst and author located in the anti-Enlightenment and anti-Science discourse/worldview/paradigm specialising in the study of the illicit drug trade, the illicit small arms trade and human smuggling of the Caribbean, Islamic extremism and racism/white supremacy with an emphasis on power relations. You can access his website to experience and download his research papers published online and view his range of books. His website address is: https://www.daurius.com and his blog on the Caribbean is at: https://drugtrade.wordpress.com/

Read more at https://www.daurius.com.

www.ingramcontent.com/pod-product-compliance
Lightning Source LLC
Chambersburg PA
CBHW031321160726
47993CB00001B/495